The Story Continues

Books by J. Ellsworth Kalas

The Parables of Paul
Heroes, Rogues, and the Rest
I Love Growing Older, But I'll Never Grow Old
A Faith of Her Own
Strong Was Her Faith
The Thirteen Apostles
Detective Stories from the Bible
Parables from the Back Side
Christmas from the Back Side

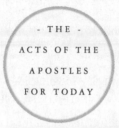

- THE -
ACTS OF THE
APOSTLES
FOR TODAY

The Story
Continues

J. ELLSWORTH KALAS

ABINGDON PRESS
NASHVILLE

THE STORY CONTINUES

Copyright © 2016 by Abingdon Press

Library of Congress Cataloging-in-Publication Data

Names: Kalas, J. Ellsworth, 1923-
Title: The story continues : the Acts of the Apostles for today / J. Ellsworth Kalas.
Description: First [edition]. | Nashville, Tennessee : Abingdon Press, 2016.
Identifiers: LCCN 2015035979 | ISBN 9781501816642 (binding: pbk.)
Subjects: LCSH: Bible. Acts—Criticism, interpretation, etc.
Classification: LCC BS2625.52 .K35 2016 | DDC 226.6/06—dc23 LC record available at http://lccn.loc.gov/2015035979

16 17 18 19 20 21—10 9 8 7 6 5 4 3 2 1
MANUFACTURED IN THE UNITED STATES OF AMERICA

Contents

Contents

FOREWORD

The Story Continues

When work on this book began, there was no way to know it would be Ellsworth Kalas's last, completed in the year of his death in November 2015 at the age of ninety-two. This great man of faith influenced the lives of so many through his preaching, pastoring, teaching, and writing.

In reflection, the topic of the Book of the Acts of the Apostles is an appropriate one for his ultimate offering. Just like the first disciples after Pentecost, Dr. Kalas was a man of both words and actions, filled and fueled by the Spirit. Even as he told and retold the stories of the Bible, he was a man who was known for acts of great love and humility, treating every person he encountered with the love of Christ.

His story continues through the impact he had on the lives of his parishioners, in the ministry of his students, and as his words continue to be read in the many books and studies that he gave us.

I met Ellsworth Kalas just before coming to study at Asbury Theological Seminary. He was a giant in the world of preaching, one of the few remaining icons of the pulpit. It's not always advisable to meet one's heroes in person.

They often fall from the pedestals imagined for them when exposed to the scrutiny of everyday life, but somehow Dr. Kalas seemed to grow in grace with every experience, every conversation. His towering stature, deep voice, and winsome countenance only contributed to his reputation as the stuff of legend. Instead of falling from grace, he only rose in my estimation as his role in my life grew from hero to teacher to friend.

Although he began preaching early, traveling as a teenage evangelist before he began a long and distinguished era in pastoral ministry, he got a late start as an author, publishing his first book at age sixty-five. After retirement (he didn't quite understand the meaning of that word), Dr. Kalas spent the last twenty plus years serving at Asbury Seminary as a distinguished professor of preaching and even, for a time, as the seminary's president.

That one of the world's greatest preachers would end up teaching beginner preaching students was both a gift and an astonishment. Imagine, if you will, that Michelangelo offered to teach an art class to kindergarteners! How could a great master of preaching bear to hear so many bad sermons? It was probably because he was motivated to make sure the Word was always preached as best it could be, with both grace and truth, and because he had a gift for helping even the worst of preachers become great.

As his student, I can tell you: when you knew you were preaching a sermon for Ellsworth Kalas, you preached better than you ever had in your life. I drew on resources I didn't even know I had within me, and I called for the

Holy Spirit's help as never before. Once I had preached in front of his class, I would collapse back into my seat, feeling that my very soul had been laid bare. And he would stand up and walk to the front of the class and say to my classmates: "And so...And so, what shall we say to Jessica about *her sermon*?" And then he would give the title—because titles were so very important to him.

My classmates would mutter a few words I barely heard, and then I would hold my breath as he began to offer his own words on what felt like Judgment Day itself. And if he said that I had done well, I felt better about myself than I ever had in my life. And if he said I had done poorly...somehow I still felt better about myself than I ever had in my life!

One of his students once asked: "How is it that he can put the knife in and turn it, and we are all still smiling when we walk away. Then once we get out the door we think to ourselves: *Oh! He cut me!*" He always told the truth, about sermons and everything else, but you always felt that he loved you still. Sometimes in our minds, his former students still hear those words after we preach a sermon: "And so, what shall we say to Nolan, to Alicia, to Steve?" We're all still trying to live up to the best that he believed about us.

He gave strong words of correction with the same love and grace that he gave words of affirmation. That gift of words was so powerful. He knew how to use his gift of words for good both in and out of the pulpit. It was his gift of written words through his published works that brought him into the homes and churches of thousands of people he never met.

Although he didn't publish his first book until he was sixty-five, he didn't let that slow him down. He came into our churches in studies like DISCIPLE Bible Study, *Christian Believer*, and *The Grand Sweep*. He came into our personal reading with his unique take on Scripture that had him approaching the Bible from a different angle: *Parables from the Back Side, New Testament Stories from the Back Side, Christmas from the Back Side*. He joked that he never expected to become so well-known for his backside.

He was a man of priceless words because he was a man of *the* Word. And the way he engaged us with Scripture has forever deepened and matured not only individual believers but also entire churches, and the Church as a whole. We are forever grateful.

When people inevitably tried to publicly recognize his greatness, he waved off all the accolades while continuing to point us to the greatness of God. The more importance the world assigned him, the more time he spent with the common person. The more that people called for him to speak and write, the more he spent time listening. The more we put him on pedestals, the more he stooped to care for the least and last among us.

It's difficult to know that these will be the last of his published words. But at the same time, he would remind us (as he does in these pages) that the story continues. And what a grand story it is.

And so. And so, what shall we say to Ellsworth Kalas about a life well-lived, well-loved, words shared, songs sung, stories told, people blessed and blessed and blessed? What shall we say?

Well done, good and faithful servant. Well done.

Jessica LaGrone
December 2015

Some Extraordinary, Unremarkable People

Once upon a time, roughly twenty centuries ago, there were some very special people on our planet. There weren't many of them, and at first glance they didn't seem very special. In truth, even a second or third glance doesn't uncover anything overly impressive. We humans shop for people in roughly the same way as we shop for clothing, groceries, and gadgets. We want people who attract us, impress us, and who look as if somehow they might benefit us. Such persons attract us by their physical appearance, their bearing, self-assurance, and personality. They impress us by their intelligence and their achievements; and if we are more discerning, by their character. And they appeal to us if we feel they can do something for us. I'm not speaking of the crassness that uses people for their position or power or money, but in the sense that we feel they can fill some empty place in our lives.

What I'm preparing to say is this, that these very special people didn't have much natural appeal in the marketplace of people shoppers. I wouldn't have been immediately drawn to them, and while I can't predict your judgment, I don't think you would have found them especially attractive either. They weren't as physically impressive as the Greek athletes, not as self-assured as the Roman civil servants, and not as intellectually stimulating as the Jews.

I'm speaking not out of any personal prejudice because I have no basis for even superficial judgment. I'm reflecting the report of a first-hand observer who was well qualified to judge, the apostle Paul. He knew these people well, and he loved them. He also knew the general culture of the times, so he was able to see them comparatively. He wrote,

> Look at your situation when you were called, brothers and sisters! By ordinary human standards not many were wise, not many were powerful, not many were from the upper class. But God chose what the world considers foolish to shame the wise. God chose what the world considers weak to shame the strong. And God chose what the world considers low-class and low-life—what is considered to be nothing—to reduce what is considered to be something to nothing. (1 Corinthians 1:26-28)

Nevertheless, when this body of people was still in the first generation of its existence some of their enemies said they were "turning the world upside down" (Acts 17:6

NRSV). The people who said this were perhaps alarmists who were overestimating trouble. But if they were poor descriptors, they were remarkable prophets.

Look at it this way. At the time those words were spoken, the world Christian population numbered in a few thousands, scattered over a wide area. Today many megachurches and a large number of metropolitan Roman Catholic parishes claim comparable numbers, and more. True, there's a huge difference between the population of the first- and twenty-first-century worlds. But put it statistically: at the time the Epistles were written, Christians would not have numbered 1 percent of the world population; today they constitute fully one-third—that is, today they number more than two billion people.

Or measure this way. Today, in a world that makes much of brand symbols, the most widely known symbol in the world is not the winsome cursive of Coca-Cola, but the cross—and this, even though in many places in our world the Christian symbol is outlawed. Remember, too, that the most widely circulated document in the world is not a political, economic, or military document but the book of this people, the Bible. And add to that the fact that literally hundreds of the world's languages are in written form today because the descendants of that little first-century movement have put spoken dialects into written form so they could make their document—or at least parts of it—available to as many people as possible. Preferably, the whole world! Indeed, this is one of their ultimate goals.

It all began with this little body of people. How did they do it? What was their secret?

It's important to realize how much the odds were against them. Christianity began as a Jewish sect; that's how the culture at large saw them, because at the first they were all Jews, by ethnic heritage or by religious conversion. And although the Jewish religious leadership itself rejected them, these first believers had their roots in Judaism, so that their first document, and their only document for at least a generation, was the Holy Scriptures of Judaism—what we now call the Old Testament. In the first-century world the Jews were respected for their intelligence and their business skills, but they were outsiders. They chose to be. The Roman Empire offered a good deal of religious freedom as long as its adherents accepted the idea that Caesar was one of the gods. Devout Jews believed there was only one God, so they were seen as religious fanatics and as proper objects of persecution. The first-century world identified Christians as Jews, but as a still more radical subset among the Jews. This wasn't an easy sell in the world of religion. This, however, was the public perception of Christians before further questions were asked. No wonder, then, that this movement called Christians, or "people of the Way," had so much going against it and so little going for it.

Worse, the subject of Christian preaching was a Galilean teacher who had been publicly executed as an enemy of the state. To affiliate with such a person was to court trouble. The believers joyfully declared that this Jesus had been raised from the dead on the third day of his entombment;

this was impressive if you accepted it, but obviously not everyone (probably not many) was likely to do so.

I should also remind us that when the movement's starting lineup came running on the field, there was no reason for a burst of hopeful applause. They were short one person to begin with because one had defected before they even got started. At least four of the eleven remaining were fishermen; this was an honorable occupation, but not much of a training program for future religious leaders. Another was a tax collector, which was a despised role in the Roman culture because it offered so many opportunities for financial scandal. Still another had been part of a failed, small-time revolutionary group. Of the rest we know nothing, which is probably significant: that is, that there was nothing memorable about them.

So how is it that with such a start this group survived—particularly since it was an object of intermittent and often brutal persecution—and exists still today?

The answer is in the Book of Acts. This candid, unvarnished account tells us how it all began and how its founders led the way—sometimes fumbling and stumbling—into greatness. I believe that their story can show us how we might, two millennia later, carry on in the same remarkable fashion.

The author lets us know at the outset that he is writing a continued story. Acts was written by the person who wrote the third Gospel, Luke. Luke was a Greek, and thus to our knowledge the only Gentile writer of a New Testament book. He was a physician and a learned man.

He traveled with Paul, apparently for extended periods. It's altogether possible that sometime in his life, Luke was a slave. When the Roman army conquered an area it customarily brought back some of the most talented people—teachers, doctors, lawyers, accountants—to serve in the households of government officials and other well-to-do persons. Luke may have been such.

See how Luke begins the Book of Acts. He addresses the book to Theophilus, just as he did with the Gospel that preceded it. Now he reminds his readers that in his "first scroll" he had written "everything Jesus did and taught from the beginning, right up to the day when he was taken up into heaven" (1:1-2). With this scroll, the Acts, he intends to continue the story.

The Gospel of Luke could well have been called "The Acts of Jesus" since that's the story it tells. This continuing story, the Book of Acts, is titled "The Acts of the Apostles." Luke perceives it to be, in the truest sense, a continuation of the Acts of Jesus. We will never do justice to the Book of Acts until we understand that those first believers understood that they were carrying on the work Jesus had begun, and that they felt he was as significantly present with them after he had ascended into heaven as when he was standing in arm's reach. Put it this way: in the Gospels, Jesus Christ is a person who *did* things; in the Book of Acts, he is a person who *does* things. In the first book Luke wrote, the one we call his Gospel, he reports on Jesus in bodily form, the person of flesh and blood who walked among the people teaching and doing good; in his sequel, the Book of Acts,

Jesus is present in the ministry of the <u>Holy Spirit</u>, and the body Jesus now inhabits is the Church that bears his name.

Jesus had promised his disciples that this would be so. On the night before his crucifixion Jesus told his disciples, "I assure you that whoever believes in me will do the works that I do. They will do even greater works than these because I am going to the Father" (John 14:12). After Jesus went to the Father, the Holy Spirit came into the world to inhabit every believer. As a physical person Jesus could be present in only one place, now he could be present wherever the church, via his followers, was present.

As we read Acts, we realize that this is how the early church saw itself. No wonder the book is called "Acts" because there's *action* in this book. Acts offers very little teaching, at least in direct fashion, but it gives us a great deal of action. When Clarence Jordan did his "Cotton Patch Version" of parts of the New Testament a generation ago, he titled Acts, appropriately, "The Happenings." It is a book of crowds and excitement, of mobs and miracles, of confrontations, arrests, persecutions, and healings, and along the way, some dangerous sea voyages. There's hardly a quiet moment in the record. Something was always happening, and the followers of Jesus felt that these happenings were occurring not only in their physical world, but also in the world of spiritual activity.

During World War II, J. B. Phillips, an Anglican rector who was serving a church in Greater London, sought to sustain his congregation during the months of horrendous, nightly bombings by teaching them the New Testament. In order to make the Bible as accessible as possible, Phillips began to make his own translation into modern English—a translation that eventually not only swept the British Isles but became widely popular in America. As Dr. Phillips translated Acts from the Greek into contemporary English he wrote, "No one can read this book [that is, Acts] without being convinced that there is Someone here at work besides mere human beings....Consequently it is a matter of sober historical fact that never before has any small body of ordinary people so moved the world."[1]

Notice that word *ordinary* because that word is key to all that happened in the first century and ever since. By almost any human standard the first leaders of this movement were not great men, not shapers of destiny. They were altogether average. I sometimes plead with my seminary students not to settle for mediocrity in their work; that is, not to be content to be average. Yet the people who laid the foundation of the church were, of themselves, quite average. Nevertheless, they *did* shape destiny. Thus, Dr. Phillips' phrase: "there is Someone here at work besides mere human beings."

Note, too, that these people were working with ordinary, everyday language. They delivered the story of Christ and the church in Greek, which was the prevalent language at that time. At one level of usage, Greek was the language of philosophers, historians, playwrights, and poets, memorable for its beauty. But those who wrote the New Testament couched it in what scholars call the *koine*: the *common* Greek of the marketplace. However, the message they conveyed was so elevated that it is no exaggeration to say that portions of it are still today the most quoted phrases on our planet.

What was the secret of these generally unremarkable men and women so that still today, nearly twenty centuries later, we feel the tidal pull of their lives? J. B. Phillips adds to my question when he comments on the title of Acts. We call this book "The Acts of the Apostles," but Phillips notes that this is something of a mistranslation. No articles are present in the Greek. Thus, if translated literally, the title would be "Acts of Apostles"—or to put the matter more clearly, "Some Acts of Some Apostles." We should remind ourselves that after the opening chapter only three of the original disciples are mentioned: Peter, James, and John. And of those three, only Peter has any measurable role in Acts. The "apostles" whose "acts" are recorded in this book are thus an almost entirely new group. Acts is not the story of an exclusive group of miracle men, but a selection of events from what was happening to many followers of Jesus: some "extraordinary, unremarkable people," to use the language of our chapter title.

But here is what we must say for the apostles, for we will never understand their story if we forget it: they knew who they were, and they knew from whence they got their strength. Soon after the Day of Pentecost, while the nature of their new life was still largely unknown territory, Peter and John came upon a man "crippled since birth" (Acts 3:2) who sought alms daily at a gate of the temple. When he asked a gift from the disciples, "Peter and John stared at him" (3:4). Ponder that simple phrase. Did they, in that moment of staring, recall what Jesus would do at such a time if he were there? And did they ponder if indeed they were now to do what their Lord had done? It seems, indeed, that they saw even more. Most of Jesus' healings came when people asked his help; Peter and John now dared to go a step further and volunteered their help unsought.

The man was miraculously healed. Something had happened. Jesus was still walking the streets of Jerusalem, but now in the person of his followers. The following day, when temple authorities brought Peter and John to a public hearing the august council "was caught by surprise by the confidence with which Peter and John spoke." Obviously, these men "were uneducated and inexperienced. They also recognized that they had been followers of Jesus" (4:13). The authorities came to a logical conclusion: "we need to warn them not to speak to anyone in this name" (4:17)— that is, in the name of Jesus.

Logical as their decision was, it was also quite naive. The one thing no one could do was to stop Jesus' followers from speaking in his name. The apostles had already made themselves clear: "Salvation can be found in no one else," they told the council. "Throughout the whole world, no other name has been given among humans through which we must be saved" (4:12).

The authorities were nonplussed. They had eliminated Jesus, but now they had a multiplied problem. Two fishermen were fearless before them, and the sympathy of the crowds was obviously with the fishermen. The council leaders did what they could: "They threatened them further, then released them" (4:21). As for the apostles and their band of enthusiastic supporters, they were so possessed by their calling that they saw no reason to fear. Instead, they prayed: "Now, Lord, take note of their threats and enable your servants to speak your word with complete confidence" (4:29). As the gathering dismissed, "they were all filled with the Holy Spirit and began speaking God's word with confidence" (4:31).

If we had been there, you and I, but not knowing what we know today, I suspect we would have been bemused. We would have agreed that it was exciting to see these unlikely people so completely taken by their convictions. But we would probably have concluded that the odds were entirely against them. They were such a collection of ordinary people (sometimes less than ordinary). They seemed like pleasant bumpkins compared to the scholars on the Hebrew council. The Roman government would put up with them as long as they didn't become unduly insistent, but if they left no room for Caesar as God, the government would dispose of them quickly. It would be only a matter of time until these Galileans were among the forgotten revolutionaries of the first century.

What Rome did not know, busy as it was with administering its empire and enjoying its privileges, and what the Hebrew council did not know, in the confidence of its learning, was that these unremarkable people were altogether extraordinary, in an out-of-this-world sort of way. Jesus the Christ had been crucified, then raised from the dead, and was now present in these unlikely people. Wherever they went (and soon you would find them almost everywhere), Jesus Christ was somehow present. The Gospel of Luke, with its acts of Jesus Christ, had now become the Acts of Christ, through the people who dared to bear his name.

2

Then There Was Pentecost

L et's say it again. Those first Christians whose story comes to us in the Book of Acts were a special kind of people. They were largely from the poorer classes of society; they possessed little or no power or influence; they were tradesmen, craftsmen, slaves, and many of them only partially employed; the majority was educated for little more than their daily work. Yet they turned the world in a new direction. And they did so in the name of a Jewish carpenter-teacher who had recently been executed as an enemy of society. What was the secret?

Acts doesn't leave us in the dark. Two things made the difference. The first was the resurrection of Jesus. Those first believers were a resurrection people. They celebrated that fact not once a year on an Easter day, but before long on the first day of the week, on what we now call Sunday. Since their heritage was in the Hebrew Scriptures, it was natural for them to worship on the seventh day of the week, the Sabbath, but in time they moved naturally to their day of wonder and victory, the first day of the week—resurrection day. Still more, however, they knew the resurrection as a fact of life that seemed to bring all others under its sway. If their Lord had conquered death, the rest of daily life was wrapped in hope.

The second factor was the coming of the Holy Spirit. Jesus told his disciples that it was better for them that he go away, because after his departure they would receive the Holy Spirit. I'm sure this was hard for them to believe—and hard for us, too. We sentimentalize about how wonderful it would be if Jesus were in our midst. Jesus would tell us, as he told his disciples, "That's the point. I *am* in your midst, if you will receive me in the presence and power of the Holy Spirit."

Jesus' last instruction to his disciples before his ascension was that they should wait in the city of Jerusalem until they had received "what the Father had promised." When they interrupted with their earnest question, "Lord, are you going to restore the kingdom to Israel now?" Jesus advised that this was none of their concern. "Rather," he said, "you will receive power when the Holy Spirit has come upon you, and you will be my witnesses in Jerusalem, in all Judea and Samaria, and to the end of the earth" (Acts 1:4, 6, 8).

To their credit, the disciples took Jesus at his word. They got an "upstairs room" in Jerusalem and began to meet. Essentially they took up residence in that room. They conducted several matters of business, particularly naming a replacement for Judas. There were only about 120 of them, so they simply constituted a Committee of the Whole. They had remarkable unity of spirit, held together by their common love for Christ.

For some ten days they met in this fashion, with prayer and worship woven through all else they were doing. Then, on the Day of Pentecost, a key festival day in the Hebrew tradition, a miracle occurred. "Suddenly a sound from heaven like the howling of a fierce wind filled the entire house where they were sitting. They saw what seemed to be individual flames of fire alighting on each one of them. They were all filled with the Holy Spirit and began to speak in other languages as the Spirit enabled them to speak" (Acts 2:2-4).

It was dramatic, and it was power-filled. Apparently the speaking in tongues continued for some time. Before long, crowds gathered to observe the phenomenon, and as they did, the group moved downstairs where they were in reach of the people. As I've indicated, Pentecost was a holiday that brought thousands of Jews to their holy city. The Pentecost holiday may have been the biggest event of the year in attendance because the season was favorable to travel.

What astonished the visiting pilgrims and quickly swelled their numbers was 120's manner of speaking. "They were mystified because everyone heard them speaking in their native languages" (Acts 2:6). The message was clear: "the mighty works of God" (2:11). And no wonder they asked, "What does this mean?" (2:12). No wonder, too, that among those who were astonished there were also scoffers who found an easy, discrediting explanation: "They're full of new wine" (2:13).

Note the honesty and integrity of the author. Someone who was hoping to prove a point would have left the impression that everyone was convinced. Luke aims to give us the facts. He finds the facts convincing enough in themselves, without adornment or selective treatment. In reporting this mixed reaction he also prepares us for what will happen through the rest of the story—not only in Acts, but into our present century. The work of the church, even in times of its greatest effectiveness, always elicits a mixed response. Some will be convinced, and some will scoff.

Luke gives us statistics to measure the day's wonders. The crowd that had gathered out of curiosity stayed to hear Peter preach. The old Peter was often loquacious, but now he was eloquent and power-filled. He took his text from the Old Testament prophet Joel, who had promised that someday God's Spirit would be poured out "on all people" (2:17). Then he reminded his audience of what they had done in crucifying Jesus some weeks earlier and quoted from the Psalms to help them grasp the resurrection. His hearers were "deeply troubled." "Brothers, what should we do?" they asked. Peter had a ready reply. "Change your hearts and lives. Each of you must be baptized in the name of Jesus Christ for the forgiveness of your sins. Then you will receive the gift of the Holy Spirit" (2:37-38). That day, Luke reports, "about three thousand people" joined the community of faith (2:41). And they did so in the name of the man they had executed.

It was an altogether astonishing day. The disciples had come out of hiding to challenge those who had crucified their Lord. The 120 had in one sermon been multiplied by twenty-five. The daring band was commanding everyone to seek forgiveness of sins and to be publicly baptized and thus to join their body. If they did, Peter promised, they too would "receive the gift of the Holy Spirit." It's hard to imagine a more complete turn-around in such a brief period of time.

This was only the beginning. Luke proceeds in a paragraph to describe the continuing scene, with day-by-day idylls of the beloved community. The believers "devoted themselves to the apostles' teaching" and to one another; they shared their meals and their prayers. "A sense of awe came over everyone. God performed many wonders and signs through the apostles." They "were united and shared everything," to the extent that if they sold some property they would bring the proceeds to help those who were in need. "Every day, they met together in the temple and ate in their homes. They shared food with gladness and simplicity," praising God and demonstrating God's goodness to everyone. And they grew. "The Lord added daily to the community those who were being saved" (2:42-47).

It's a breathtaking sequence. If it were to happen today, I'm not sure I'd be ready for it. Theirs was a communitarian society, and the introvert in me wants a little more space for myself. As it turns out, however, neither did the early church make this a permanent characteristic of their body. Mind you, over the centuries the church has had numbers of communitarian bodies, ranging from the varieties of monastic orders to Protestant groups like the Herrnhut community, but such communitarianism has never since characterized the entire body.

Instead, the time was shortly to come when this wonderfully tight-knit Jerusalem group would be driven into "all the world," to be the salt of the earth that God had called them to be. Our challenge is to see how we can keep the spirit that pervaded the first church—the "wonders and signs," the "gladness and simplicity," the sense of unity and glad sharing, and the quality of life that "demonstrated God's goodness to everyone" (2:47). This was the spirit in which the church was born, and the spirit which made it possible for the Lord to add to its numbers daily.

Let's go back to review what happened on the Day of Pentecost. When the 120 first gathered, there was a sense of caution and fear, and with good reason. They had come together because all they had was one another, their common love for Jesus Christ, and their knowledge that he had been raised from the dead. Jesus had made clear that they were to go into all the world with their message, but they had no idea how to do so. They must also have wondered how it could be that thousands had heard their Lord teach and preach and had observed his miracles, and that now all that was left was such a pathetically small number.

But they also knew that their Lord had told them to "wait for what the Father had promised" because "in only a few days you will be baptized with the Holy Spirit" (1:4-5). So they waited! There's such a thing as active waiting. Expectant, powerful waiting, that makes possible that for which we wait. When the transforming hour came, it was dramatic. First, "the howling of a fierce wind" that filled the house. Then, "what seemed to be individual flames of fire alighting on each one of them." And then, they were "filled with the Holy Spirit and began to speak in other languages as the Spirit enabled them to speak" (2:2-4).

Almost certainly this initial group was composed entirely of Jews. They saw everything through the prism of their Hebrew Scriptures. Whatever other limitations might have handicapped this little group, they knew their basic document, the books of the Law and the prophets. Thus, as we have noted, when Peter stood up to explain to the crowd what was happening, he drew immediately on Joel's prophecies. So, too, with the symbols of Pentecost. *Wind* was for them a word used interchangeably with *spirit*. Thus at creation it was "God's wind [that] swept over the waters" (Genesis 1:2). At the conclusion of the flood, "God sent a wind over the earth so that the waters receded" (8:1).

The sound at Pentecost was "like the howling of a fierce wind," so powerful that it filled the entire house where the 120 were gathered (Acts 2:2). God's wind, the Spirit, had *filled* the gathering place, crowding out all competing forces. I'm sure that on occasions God's Spirit is a gentle breeze of comfort, but at Pentecost it was a ruthless invasion. A new time had come for the people and the purposes of God. In the Old Testament the Spirit of God came upon

19

special people—prophets, priests, judges, and kings—to equip them for their assignments, but at Pentecost God's Wind came for all who would receive—including at times the reluctant, the doubtful, and the rebellious—and it is *fierce* in asserting its right.

Then there were "individual flames of fire alighting on each one of them" (2:3). These Jews knew about the divine fire. Fire consumed the whole burnt offerings in the tabernacle and the temple. It was fire that vindicated the prophet Elijah when he dared to challenge the pagan priests who had been influencing Israel. And when the prophet Isaiah realized that he was "ruined," because he was "a man with unclean lips" living "among a people with unclean lips," God met his need by a "glowing coal that he had taken from the altar with tongs" (Isaiah 6:5-6).

A new thing was happening, and God's Spirit was employing familiar symbols to connect the new with the old. The fire symbol also related with John the Baptist's announcement about Christ: "he will baptize you with the Holy Spirit and with fire"—"a fire that can't be put out" (Matthew 3:11-12). And with these symbols there was the speaking in tongues, so that those in the crowd heard "the mighty works of God in our own languages" (Acts 2:11)!

As the Holy Spirit continued to come upon believers in the Book of Acts, neither the wind nor the fire is mentioned. Nor is the speaking in tongues of the same nature. When Peter preached to Cornelius's gathering the Spirit fell upon the group so that they spoke "in other languages…praising God" (10:46), but not in the sense of their being witnesses to the faith. One notes, too, that when the Ethiopian eunuch was so marvelously converted through the witness of Philip, there was no reference to an infilling of the Holy Spirit, though surely God's Spirit was wonderfully at work (8:26-40).

In our day any discussion of the Day of Pentecost and of the work of the Holy Spirit must include reference to what we currently know as the "charismatic" or "Pentecostal" movement. This movement includes great numbers of Roman Catholics as well as persons in almost every Protestant body. They are the most rapidly growing religious movement in the world, numbering some five hundred million persons—that is, nearly a quarter of those who identify themselves as Christians. They are only loosely organized except for specific Pentecostal denominations, and no doubt a great many people practice the "gift of tongues" privately without associating themselves publicly in any way.

Their experience relates to the Day of Pentecost, though not in the sense of evangelizing by speaking miraculously in a language unknown to them in order to convert others. Rather, they are like the persons Paul addresses in his First Letter to the Corinthians who found personal spiritual vitality in tongues—in our day, especially in what many call their "prayer language." This experience has brought new vitality to many twenty-first-century believers. Like any expressions of religion, it can be—and is—sometimes abused. Many overemphasize its importance. But it is impressive for the new life it brings to many otherwise casual believers.

The proof of the Holy Spirit's presence in our lives is not by a sign of fire or a rushing wind, nor speaking in tongues, but in the quality of our Christian living. The New Testament pleads for believers to have the *fruit* of the Spirit: "love, joy, peace, patience, kindness, goodness, faithfulness, gentleness, and self-control" (Galatians 5:22-23). These are common words in our vocabulary of human living at its best, but it is clear that the apostle has a more than ordinary quality in mind. He perceives Christians as possessing these virtues at a beyond-human-attainment level, a level possible only by an extraordinary work of the Holy Spirit in our personal lives.

Is it possible for anyone to live in such rarefied spiritual air in our sometimes stifling secular culture? Could we quite ordinary mortals be so Spirit-filled that we would devote ourselves to knowing the Scriptures (more than sports statistics, political and economic jargon, and popular gossip that preoccupy us), sharing meals and prayers, living with a sense of awe, uniting and sharing everything, after making a gain in stocks or in property transactions choosing to give it away—that is, so to live that our daily lives become a demonstration of God's goodness to everyone? (Acts 2:42-47). In other words, to become a Christlike influence in the daily life of our time and place?

The answer, of course, is that our times are against it. If you're candid, you may advise me that my question isn't even realistic.

I agree. It's as unrealistic as if someone had raised the same question in the first-century world of the Book of Acts. There, too, everything was against such a radical way of life. In our time people are amused at the idea of such religious enthusiasm. In the first century, you might have been arrested for it and brought to trial. Nevertheless, it happened. The evidence is in the Book of Acts—and indeed, in the fact that at this moment we're reading and discussing a book written about what happened then. We wouldn't be doing so if it weren't that some people twenty centuries ago were so deeply and radically convinced that the tide of its influence is with us still.

So we're back to the question: Could it happen today? Could the church once again become such a vital institution that some would fear we were turning the world upside down?

We can engage in this study with one of two approaches. It can be an earnest, vigorous study of a historical event in the life of the Christian church, but done in a detached way. Or we can study while constantly asking ourselves if it could ever happen again. Perhaps even now, in the twenty-first century.

Either way we will benefit by our study. But suppose, just suppose, that we would find ourselves in a new birth of the church, one that—with regard to differences of time and personnel—would be the first-century church in the twenty-first century? What if?

3

People of the Great Heart

We don't know much about a person or an institution until we see what can happen when such a person or body comes to recognize its own potential. Thus far in our study of Acts we have made much of how limited were the resources of the early company of believers. Our analysis is correct, as far as it has gone. If we're familiar with the story of Jesus and his disciples, we know that by most standards of judgment the core group with which Jesus worked for three years had apparently modest potential. There were some diamonds in the rough, but the roughness was more apparent than the diamond flash. That's why it's so difficult to name more than four or five of the original disciples.

But on the Day of Pentecost there were some three thousand converts, and every day that followed, more converts came. Only a few of these persons are known to us by name; one wonders about the others. No doubt most of them were what we're inclined to call "average people" or "everyday folks." But the longer I live with the Gospel of grace, the more cautious I am about calling any person "average." No one can estimate what can happen to an individual or to an institution when the Spirit of God is given reign. Perhaps that's why the apostle Paul was so casual if not careless in referring to his people as *saints*. He knew the potential that lies in every redeemed soul.

Luke is still summarizing what happened on the Day of Pentecost when he gives us further insight into the possibilities in the growing company of converts. He tells us of their joy, their hunger for teaching, their devotion to prayer, and the awe that pervaded their gatherings. And then, a specific kind of measurement, the kind that business institutions and accountants can measure. "All the believers were united and shared everything" (Acts 2:44). This is a lovely statement, but rather general. The following sentence is more business-like, more statistically real: "They would sell pieces of property and possessions and distribute the proceeds to everyone who needed them" (2:45).

This is an electric statement. For one, it indicates that some of the new believers had a measure of financial security: "property and possessions." This means that there were landowners among them. Possessions? Jewels were among the most notable and, of course, also cattle and sheep. We don't know how much these people had, but here's the important point: their new faith gave them a new view of their possessions. The miser never has enough, and cautious persons often edge closer to miserliness than they would want to confess. By contrast, the redeemed get a larger view of their resources; they see that they have more than they realized. With it, they see ways to give that they hadn't recognized before. A converted heart gives us a godly ability to see our resources for purposes of giving.

This quality burst forth with beauty in the first-century church. Believers saw that they had more than they had previously understood. They had a new sense of economics. They possessed the spirit of the Sermon on the Mount, where Jesus tells us that we ought to worry less about *things*: after all, even Solomon wasn't as wonderfully adorned as the lilies of the field, where the providing is in God's hands. Believers also gain a new sensitivity to the needs of other people. "I didn't know there was so much need in the world" is often the phrase of the new convert or the person who has made a mission trip to some other part of the world (which in some cases may be a neighborhood in the same city where they've lived for years).

This is something of the spirit behind the generosity that broke forth in the early church. So it is still when God's Spirit touches some heretofore dull corner of any life. These exuberant believers "shared everything." They did so "with gladness and simplicity." And when they looked at a piece of property they realized how much they had and, in another moment, how much someone needed what they had. Redeemed vision does remarkable things to what we see in our possessions and in how we see the needs of others.

27

This is one of the most telling facts about the quality of the early church, but one to which we have given little attention. We read about their miracles and wonder if miracles are real and, if so, how they can fit into our time and place. We see spiritual gifts at work and raise questions about fanaticism or the significance for our times. But in the way the early Christians looked at their money and used it, we have a very everyday, wonderfully practical demonstration of Christianity at work. Here is a miracle to which we should give greater attention because at a bedrock level few matters are more miraculous than a new attitude toward our possessions. Perhaps we miss the wonder in this part of the story and its beauty because it is so close to home. If we think about it too much, it becomes troublesome. Sometimes we're more comfortable with theological questions that are remote. Our use of money, however, is simple and immediately within our daily reach. This makes it troublesome. We like remote problems better, and remote miracles, too.

This grace of joyous generosity was an earmark of the first believers. It dominates Luke's one paragraph summary of what characterized the first days following Pentecost. Perhaps we should give it some of the time we ordinarily devote to discussions about speaking in tongues and other such manifestations of the Holy Spirit. It was spontaneous, a natural response to one's possessions and to another's need. It wasn't organized! Apparently there was no system of evaluating entitlement: they gave "the proceeds to everyone who needed them" (2:45). The skeptical among us wonder how often this generosity was abused by those who might be inclined to take advantage of their neighbors. All we know at this point in the story is that the newly-filled souls had a new attitude toward worldly goods and human need. The giving was marked by joy and by a new sensitivity to the needs of others.

Before long, we meet a particular person who became the embodiment of this spirit (just as, not long after, we meet a couple who violated its beauty). The embodiment was that remarkable man, Joseph of Cyprus, who is known to us primarily by his nickname, Barnabas. It comes early in the Acts story. Once again Luke is telling us about the remarkable spirit in the company of believers. It's as if he can't get over the wonder of it. "None of them would say, 'This is mine!' about any of their possessions, but held everything in common." He interrupts this report long enough to tell us that the "apostles continued to bear powerful witness to the resurrection of the Lord Jesus, and an abundance of grace was at work among them all" (4:32-33), then returns to this sense of wonder: "There were no needy persons among them" (4:34). Why? Because of this extraordinary practice of selling property and bringing the proceeds to "the care and under the authority of the apostles" (4:35). Some sense of structure is coming into place; someone is responsible to receive the money and to distribute it, and it is the apostles, at that time, twelve specific persons. The apostles "distributed to anyone who was in need" (4:35).

It's here that we meet Joseph of Cyprus, whose monetary gift was apparently one of the largest (perhaps the very largest) received, but whose spirit was still more remarkable. He "owned a field, sold it, brought the money, and placed it in the care and under the authority of the apostles" (4:37). He was "nicknamed Barnabas (that is, 'one who encourages')" (4:36), or "son of encouragement" (4:36 NRSV).

No one ever had a finer or more fitting nickname. Almost surely he was one of those persons who came into the new body of believers on the Day of Pentecost. For devout Jews, it was important to attend at least one of the traditional annual festivals. Since he was from the island of Cyprus, he had made a substantial journey to reach Jerusalem, but since he was a person of substance, he could afford the trip.

It may seem surprising that Barnabas was a landowner since he was a Levite. Under the Old Testament law a Levite could not own property. But by the first century many Levites did, and some because of their political connections were quite well to do. We have no idea whether Barnabas had any earlier exposure to Jesus as a teacher, though it seems unlikely since his residence was in Cyprus. More likely he was one of those several thousand who first heard the message via the Pentecost outpouring, when they testified that they heard these ecstatic witnesses "declaring the mighty works of God in our own languages" (2:11)!

We don't know when Joseph of Cyprus was nicknamed Barnabas. We know that it was relatively common in the first century to nickname people by personal attributes. It's possible that fellow believers attached this descriptive name to Barnabas as a result of this very gift; after all, Luke is reporting the story several years later, after the nickname had become by common usage the name by which most people knew Joseph of Cyprus.

As the story of the early church unfolds, Barnabas becomes a key personality in the church. In drama of stage and screen there are lead characters and major supporting roles. Put Barnabas near the top of those with major supporting roles. By his nature he seems to have enjoyed giving opportunity to others; thus, "encourager" rather than "commander" is the nickname his fellow believers gave him.

At this point Barnabas encouraged by way of his wealth. Later he does so by his influence and by the very quality of his character. We too often measure wealth primarily by economic data, but all of us have wealth beyond such measurements: our influence, our sensitivity, our intelligence and creativity, and our readiness to be concerned for others.

But the major factor at this point in the life of the early church is in their financial generosity. It impresses the author of Acts, Luke, so that he gives this factor in the church particular attention. He was right to do so, and in doing so he was reflecting the teachings of Jesus. It is significant that Jesus wove parables around the theme of employers and their stewards, making the point that the stewards were being judged on the way they handled the resources—money and property—entrusted to them.

Money and other possessions have power. Indeed, the other gifts we humans enjoy—our talents, our intelligence, our creativity—eventually are translated into financial terms. Whether it is an athlete's ability on the playing field; an entertainer's skill on the stage; the creativity of the composer, writer, or inventor; or another person's managerial or administrative skills, ultimately we decide how much money these powers are worth. Even—especially!—we pay money for something as intangible as personality and, indeed, character and trustworthiness.

It's easy to lament the power of money and possessions, but they have become the measure of so much of life. And in some measure they always have—ever since someone with one sheep envied the person who had two.

No wonder, then, that Jesus issued such a truly frightening warning. "I assure you that it will be very hard for a rich person to enter the kingdom of heaven. In fact, it's easier for a camel to squeeze through the eye of a needle than for a rich person to enter God's kingdom" (Matthew 19:23-24). We're quick to admire the figure of speech Jesus used and then to forget the point. His first audience, the twelve disciples, was wiser. They knew the power of money; even as modest businessmen they dealt with the issue every day—and no doubt often envied those who were more richly endowed. So "they were stunned. 'Then who can be saved?' they asked" (19:25).

Obviously, the disciples believed in the power of money. They calculated instinctively that those who had more had the best chance of being saved because their success seemed to indicate that they already had God's favor. At this point, "Jesus looked at them carefully and said, 'It's impossible for human beings. But all things are possible for God' " (19:25-26). That is, it is exceedingly difficult for the rich to be saved—a miracle, veritably!—but "all things are possible for God."

Now, as the church is coming into its fullness in Acts, these same apostles find themselves presiding over a miracle: people with possessions are being saved! The possessions probably ranged from a piece of jewelry that had been passed on in the family to the substantial landowner. Whoever and whatever, the holdings were being translated into the coin of Caesar's kingdom and from there to the service of the Kingdom of Love.

What I like about all of this is not the money, but the spirit. The *Holy Spirit*, in fact. The people who had come to know Christ looked at their resources in an entirely different way. They were now much better economists because they saw the power of their resources more clearly than ever, and they realized more dramatically how much had been entrusted to them. Most important, they saw how much good they could do with it, and they discovered how exciting it was to get the true worth out of their resources.

The incidents we're discussing happened in the first year or two of the life of the church. Roughly a generation later, the apostle Paul is taking up an offering in the church at Corinth for needy believers elsewhere. He reports gladly that the enthusiasm of the Corinthian believers "motivated most of them" (2 Corinthians 9:2), and he wants to be sure that the Corinthians now fulfill their earlier commitments. Paul writes carefully. "I don't want you to feel like you are being forced to give anything....Everyone should give whatever they have decided in their heart. They shouldn't give with hestitation or because of pressure. God loves a cheerful giver" (9:5, 7).

There's the key word, the Holy Spirit word: *cheerful.* Our culture teaches us that money is a serious matter. It's what will pay off our mortgage, take care of us in our old age, and cover unexpected medical bills. It sends our children to college and makes it possible to take a coveted vacation; and for some, it simply means bread on the table tomorrow. Money is serious business. You don't have to convince me because I remember sitting at a Depression Era table with my parents as they counted—literally!—nickels and pennies.

But if money is only serious business, it's no wonder that it's hard for those who are rich to get into heaven, because heaven is happy beyond imagining. If there isn't some *cheerful* note in money, it's the devil's mixture for sure.

St. Francis of Assisi was one of those souls who brought into his own time (1182?–1226) the spirit of the early church. In telling Francis's story, G. K. Chesterton noted that "the freshness and freedom of the first Christians" has seemed to succeeding ages "a lost and almost prehistoric age of gold."[1]

Chesterton's phrase is just right: an "almost prehistoric age of gold." A time, that is, when people possessed a gold beyond calculation, the gold of seeing what we have as more than a means of existence and more than a way of providing for our ever-changing desires and standards of living. Rather, the joy of loving God by way of our resources, in seeing our resources as a way of blessing all of God's creatures.

Such was the mood of the early church. I put it right up there with the gifts of the Spirit, the healing of the lame man at the gate of the temple, and the fearless energy with which the disciples declared their faith. In many ways it is the most beautiful gift of all: the gift of a grateful, generous heart.

4

And of Course There Were Hypocrites

A cynic who reads the opening chapters of Acts is likely to say, "It's too good to last." The story is too idyllic in every way. A frightened little group of people suddenly becomes a fearless body that draws thousands into its ranks. Miracles occur. Everyone loves everyone. The rule of the group is generosity, not self-seeking, and no one has to exhort in order to make it happen. Poverty is unknown among the believers because others quickly see the need and just as quickly remedy it.

Perhaps the cynic is right, because at this point hypocrisy slips in. And it slips in the front door. Hypocrisy—the bane of the church and the failure that disillusions those who are outside—appears in the church when it is at its best, just when you can't imagine it happening.

Luke is a historian and, like the best historians, a master storyteller. He has hardly finished introducing us to one of the loveliest characters in the early church and one of its most generous givers, Barnabas, when there's a simple transition word. *However*. When the scene is bad, *however* is a promising word. When the scene is good, you don't want to see *however*. Unfortunately, as surely as there is a Barnabas in the church, there will also be "a man named Ananias, along with his wife Sapphira" (Acts 5:1).

Like Barnabas, they own property. Like Barnabas, they sell it. And that's where the similarity ends. Barnabas gives all his proceeds to the church. Ananias and his wife agree privately to hold back some of the money; Ananias takes the rest to the apostles. Peter senses something in Ananias's manner. "Ananias," he asks, "how is it that Satan has influenced you to lie to the Holy Spirit by withholding some of the proceeds from the sale of your land? Wasn't that property yours to keep? After you sold it, wasn't the money yours to do with whatever you wanted? What made you think of such a thing? You haven't lied to other people but to God" (5:3-4).

When Ananias heard these words, "he dropped dead" (5:5). Some young men wrapped his body, and buried it. Three hours later, Ananias's wife, Sapphira, came, not knowing what had happened. Peter asked her if she and her husband had received a certain amount for the property. She lied. Peter asked her how she and her husband could have schemed together to challenge God's Spirit. He told her what had happened to her husband, and she too dropped dead and was buried. Not surprisingly, the event shook the church. They realized that it was serious business to lie to God. To put it another way, hypocrisy is a lie to people, but it is a lie about God and righteousness. And that's serious business, indeed.

This is a troublesome story. Hearing or reading it you may have told yourself that you can't believe God would strike somebody dead; it seems unfair and violent. Well, I read the Bible by the rule that it isn't my job to make it conform to my taste, but to try instead to see what it is saying and how therefore I ought to live.

First, let me note that the Bible doesn't say that God killed Ananias and Sapphira, but that they fell down and died. This is psychologically sound. People now and again die from sheer fright, from shock, or from fear of consequences. Ananias and Sapphira were trying to deceive in a matter that was so important to them that when they were caught, they had an attack of mind and body, and died. God didn't kill them; their own smitten hearts did.

Let me say, further, that we have long forgotten that there is an austere side to Christianity and to the love of God. We sentimentalize love, flavoring it with emotional saccharine until we hardly recognize the real article. Real love has an upright quality and a measure of severity. It gives itself without measure, and its price in return is just as absolute. One has no business dealing in love at a bargain counter, because there's no true love—divine or human—that doesn't have a demanding price.

Let's pause to point out something symbolic in this story. Ananias and Sapphira died for their hypocrisy. In truth, there's always a deadliness in hypocrisy. Persons who use religion to deceive others are guilty first of all of deceiving themselves because they've convinced themselves that the imitation is as good as the real thing. This dulls them to the convicting voice that calls us to a consistent Christian life and, therefore, always to something higher and altogether authentic. Unfortunately, if we live with hypocrisy long enough we will no longer know that we're hypocrites and that our religion is playacting. Hypocrites don't realize that they're playing for a very small audience, made up of themselves and perhaps a few sympathetic friends. No one else continues to watch their act.

Hypocrisy is such a pathetic state. The hypocrite's sense of values is out of joint. He lives for the veneer of life rather than for its substance. Ananias and Sapphira were impressed by the wrong things. They saw the admiration Barnabas received rather than the beauty of his deed and character. Thus they sought the approval of the apostles rather than approval from God. If the hypocrite worked as hard to get reality as he does to keep up an appearance, he'd no doubt become a saint.

Perhaps we wish secretly that Luke had omitted the Ananias and Sapphira story. Surely he had endless stories of people like Barnabas, the kind that would warm the heart. But Luke is an honest historian; this is why we can take Acts seriously. And Luke wants us to know that hypocrisy is no minor matter. It is *deadly*, not only to those who practice it but also to those who reject the faith because of it.

In its own untoward way, hypocrisy is a high tribute to Christianity. Whether the subject is money, jewelry, learning, culture patterns, or taste, very few pretend to be less than they are. The counterfeiter doesn't print one dollar bills. People don't boast about being elected to a club that accepts everyone. It's natural—indeed, healthy—to want to be thought well of. It's unfortunate when we pretend to be something we're not in order to win such approval.

It is also unfortunate when people evaluate Christianity by the wrong standards. There have been times in western history when people joined the church because doing so would help their business or give them social prestige or political power. As our Lord said of the first-century hypocrites, "that's the only reward they'll get" (Matthew 6:2).

The worst hypocrites in Jesus' day, the group that Jesus spoke to most severely, were the Pharisees, who had high outward standards but who tended to profess more than they lived. No one gives a worse name to religion in any form than does the hypocrite. The church has no more dangerous enemy than the hypocrite. Unfortunately, this enemy claims to belong to the body.

I'm sure I've known my share of hypocrites. Worse, I'm sure I've sometimes been a hypocrite in that I've allowed people—sometimes encouraged them!—to think better of me than I deserve. I don't think, however, that hypocrites are as plentiful among believers as is generally assumed. A hypocrite is an *intentional* deceiver: someone who tries to hide behind religion and to use it for its benefits without fulfilling its demands. This is nothing like those Christians who try faithfully to live godly lives but who fall short of their own earnest efforts.

In truth, believers who feel satisfied with their level of spiritual achievement probably have a low standard of expectation. I've known more than my share of beautiful Christians in my life, but I don't know of any who fully lived up to the standards of the Christian faith. This life is not for the faint of heart! As Jesus indicated, after we have done our best we will still recognize that we are unprofitable servants.

But this doesn't make us hypocrites. The big league shortstop who committed an error in yesterday's game is not by that error an athletic hypocrite, and the earnest journalist who mistakes a "that" for a "which" is not a hypocritical writer; it's just that they aren't yet perfect in their profession. If we are sincerely Christian we strive to be as Christ-like as possible, and the occasions when we fall short of that standard don't make us hypocrites. In no way is the church a perfect organization made up of perfect people. To the contrary, we join it because we know we're imperfect and because we hope by God's strength to become better. We may fail often, and sometimes badly. We may, indeed, fail at the same testing place repeatedly. But these failures don't mark us as hypocrites. Rather, they indicate that we're on the road to sainthood, and that we're finding—as have twenty centuries before us—that this is not an easy road. To be a hypocrite is to profess goodness which we do not possess and which probably we aren't very earnestly seeking, in order to deceive other people. A hypocrite is trying to impress people, while the true believer is hoping to please God—and as much as is possible, not disappoint the people who trust him or her.

But what shall the church do when it has real hypocrites? And of course there are some; nothing is more worth "counterfeiting" than Christianity, so there will always be hypocrites. What can we do about it? I hasten to say that I'm not hoping for a reenactment of the Ananias and Sapphira story! We would help ourselves a great deal, however, if we defined more sharply what it means to be a Christian. We are more than a body of nice people, though no one should excel us in down-to-earth, day-by-day kindness. We are not simply an adjunct to any political party. We're not a philosophical or theological debating society.

The apostle urged Titus to teach his congregation to "be obedient and ready to do every good thing" (Titus 3:1). Over many centuries Christians have followed this counsel in impressive fashion. Whatever our failings over the centuries, we should remember that the church, both Catholic and Protestant, built hospitals, schools, orphanages, and shelters for the unwanted long before governmental bodies got involved in such matters. Nevertheless, we are more than that.

We have some particular beliefs about human beings that are outside the world of secular education. We believe that we humans are made in the image of God; made of the same stuff as the dust of the earth, but inhabited by the breath of God. More than that, we believe that our inherent value is so great in God's sight that Christ came into the world to save us; that is, that we are eternally valuable. Our value is beyond our training, our remarkable gifts, our creativity, our potential genius: we are eternal creatures. I think of the medieval monk who became seriously ill while traveling. He was under a vow of poverty, so when he was found he looked like a beggar. He recovered consciousness on an examining table where several doctors were examining him. In the manner of learned men in their time, they were discussing his case in Latin and questioned the efforts that should be made in treating him since he was obviously a common beggar. The monk replied in Latin, "Call no man common for whom Christ died." This is the essence of our biblical view of humanity. We human creatures, however depraved in mind or conduct and however limited in our obvious achievements, are nevertheless persons for whom Christ died.

The church is the only institution assigned to this prime factor in us humans. In the process of working with this eternal creature we also deal with the mind, the body, the psyche; all of life is our domain. But we alone are assigned the care of the eternal creature, and if we fail in this we have failed in our primary reason for existence. Thus our aim is exceedingly high and open to every imaginable failure of fulfillment. We should not be surprised that we often fall short of our expectation and of the expectations of our critics; we should be surprised, rather, that we manage as well as we do.

But we can't be content there. A lapse in quality is serious in any and every field, but nowhere more so than in the world of religion. By its nature, religion is judged by its moral and ethical product and when it falls short it loses all credibility. Nor does the church dare to bring down its standards. If we explain that the entire culture is in a period of decline, it is not an excuse but a further indictment of our failure, because moral and ethical issues are our specific territory.

In this, the church has a dilemma. When the church, or some segment within it, enforces a high standard, it is criticized for being "unloving." We are reminded that the church is meant to save sinners, not condemn them. The people who condemn the church for its hypocrites will speak just as critically of the church for enforcing its rules if the sin or sinner in question appeals to the critic. When general standards are going down, the church needs more than ever to be the model of all that is right.

William Lecky, the nineteenth-century landmark historian was known for his search for the "natural causes" behind theological and moral beliefs. As he surveyed the growth of Christianity in the early centuries he wrote, "One great cause of its success was that it produced more heroic actions and formed more upright men than any other creed."[1] It did so not by accommodating its standards to the prevailing culture but by calling its people to ever higher ground.

There is no further report in Acts where hypocrisy is confronted as it was with Ananias and Sapphira. Paul's letters to the Corinthians, however, show how severely the early believers confronted lapses in conduct. Paul tells his people that they are not to judge those "in the outside world" (1 Corinthians 5:10). But as for those in the church, "I'm writing to you not to associate with anyone who calls themselves 'brother' or 'sister' who is sexually immoral, greedy, someone who worships false gods, an abusive person, a drunk, or a swindler. Don't even eat with anyone like this. What do I care about judging outsiders? Isn't it your job to judge insiders? God will judge outsiders. *Expel the evil one from among you*" (5:11-13; italics in the translation).

Reading Paul's fierce words we're inclined to ask what has happened to grace. Paul would tell us that grace will be given as the sinner repents. He insists that the believer knows better than to act immorally and that such conduct destroys the church. By winking at immorality, greediness, and abusive conduct, we endorse it.

As one who was a pastor for nearly forty years and who has now been associated with a fine theological seminary for another twenty and more, I confess that I don't know how to apply the first-century standards in the twenty-first century. The biggest problem, candidly, is that in practice we are not the first-century church. We're not a movement that people join at the cost of their public standing; rather, we are a generally popular organization that very many people join in the same way they join a secular club or any other community organization. As for sin, we are quick to quote Jesus when he said to the accusers of the woman caught in adultery, "Whoever hasn't sinned should throw the first stone," and to say to the woman, "Is there no one to condemn you? Neither do I condemn you." But we forget to say, "from now on, don't sin any more" (John 8:7-11).

I know the danger in religious legalism. I know that Jesus found self-righteousness the most repugnant of sins, and when we start passing judgment on the conduct of others, we slip easily into self-righteousness. I'm altogether certain that I am not qualified to judge, but I also know that sometimes judgment must be given. But I think our answer must be found earlier in the process. That is, we're not ready to deal, from a human point of view, with Ananias and Sapphira until our church looks more like Barnabas and his kind.

5

Did the Apostles Make a Mistake?

Hypocrisy was only one of the problems when the church was young. Sometimes the first believers seemed intent on proving not only that they were human, but also that being filled with the Holy Spirit didn't prevent their having problems. However, the Spirit did help in solving their problems.

At this point in the story the church was still centered in Jerusalem, and no doubt the majority was still there. The message had gone out in every direction, but Jerusalem was the mother church and what happened there reverberated through the rest of the body.

The Jerusalem church was made up of two types of Jewish people, Palestinian Jews and Greek-speaking Jews. The Greek-speaking Jews were Jews who had been part of the diaspora; they could be found almost anywhere in the then-known world. Probably many of those in the

Jerusalem church were persons who had been converted on the Day of Pentecost and who found this experience and its fellowship so compelling that they decided to stay in Jerusalem, where they could be with their new faith family.

Palestinian Jews prided themselves on their purity of blood and language, and they were inclined to look down on Greek-speaking Jews. At worst they saw them as foreigners but at the least as persons separated in a measure from their ancient heritage. Ideally, these age-old prejudices should have been wiped out by the new experience in Christ, but when we see how strong it was in Jerusalem we understand better how clear-sighted and daring Paul was when he declared some years later, "There is neither Jew nor Greek; there is neither slave nor free; nor is there male and female, for you are all one in Christ Jesus" (Galatians 3:28). Ethnic loyalties run deep in much of the human race, as does the sound of one's native tongue. Here, early in the church's history, it asserts itself in a very human situation. And with one of these situations came some unexpected developments.

Sometimes we're disappointed—some are even cynical—that Christians are troubled by old prejudices. But Christianity is not magic. Salvation transforms our basic nature, but leaves to us the responsibility of daily decisions related to the issues in which we live out our faith. Some of the daily choices are painful. It is through such choices and decisions, however, that we grow up spiritually.

So it was that in the earliest days of the Christian community there was a misunderstanding between the Palestinian

Jews and the Greek-speaking Jews. A great many of the
Christians ate together all of the time. In the course of this
daily process the Greek-speaking group began to feel that
their widows were not being treated fairly in the daily distribution of food and supplies. It seemed to them that the
Palestinian Jews (who were no doubt a majority and also
dominant in the leadership) favored their own kind.

We can only guess how much truth there was in this
complaint. It would be natural for the Palestinian Jews to
favor the ones they knew best ("A little more for you, dear
soul"—such a lovely expression of affection for someone
you've known for years), and just as natural for Greek-
speaking Jews to see more in such gestures than was
intended. But intended or not, such special kindness could
make the Greek-speaking persons feel like outsiders, like
second-class members of this body of Christ.

Whatever the justice of the case, it was a serious problem, and the leadership was wise enough to realize how
hurtful it could be to individuals and how destructive to
the unity of the entire body. The twelve apostles called a
meeting of the entire church. "It isn't right," they said, "for
us to set aside proclamation of God's word in order to
serve tables." Rather, "we will devote ourselves to prayer
and the service of proclaiming of the word" (Acts 6:2, 4).
See their wisdom. First, they honored the apostolic office
of prayer and proclamation. It's significant that no mention is made of their administrative office—after all, they
were the ultimate decision-shaping body—but that they
measured their work by its spiritual dimensions.

Second, they saw table-waiting as crucially important. There are no unimportant jobs in the church, since every activity is in some way related to the eternal soul, whether by decisions made or opportunities ignored. For several years I accompanied seminars in Korea. On one occasion my students were able to direct questions to the pastor of the largest Methodist congregation in the world. One asked the lead pastor the secret of the strength and growth of his church. The pastor's first two points were predictable: excellent preaching and quality music. "Third," he said, "good ushers." He explained that the usher/greeter was the first official person a visitor encountered, and that this person's sensitivity, warmth, and spiritual maturity would begin to shape the newcomer's impression of the church before they heard the choir, the soloists, or the preaching. The church's "business" is eternal at every point.

So the apostles instructed the body of believers to "carefully choose" seven men who were "well-respected and endowed by the Spirit with exceptional wisdom" (6:3). The people applauded the decision and "selected Stephen, a man endowed by the Holy Spirit with exceptional faith" and six other men, including "Nicolaus from Antioch, a convert to Judaism" (6:5). The apostles laid hands of prayer on these men. Luke reports that "God's word continued to grow. The number of disciples in Jerusalem increased significantly. Even a large group of priests embraced the faith" (6:7).

At this point the story takes a dramatic turn. Let me underline that the twelve apostles (including Matthias,

Judas's successor), constituted the honored leadership of the church, and that even members of the Levitical priest-hood—persons trained by their office in Judaism for spiritual leadership—were coming into the church. The church is poised for success. And seven good men are seeing to it that the food is distributed equitably among the people. Then a new hero arises, the person ever afterward remembered as the first martyr for Christ. And it is not an apostle or a priestly convert, but one of the table waiters, Stephen.

We already knew that Stephen was "a man endowed by the Holy Spirit with exceptional faith," but who could have predicted his courage and eloquence! It began with his "doing great wonders and signs among the people" (6:8). This awakened opposition from a particular synagogue group who engaged him in a public debate. They shouldn't have tried! The people "couldn't resist the wisdom the Spirit gave him as he spoke" (6:10). They tried a trick question, then dragged him before the Jerusalem Council, the leaders of the entire Jewish community. The men in the council "stared at Stephen, and they saw that his face was radiant, just like an angel's" (6:15).

What follows is the longest single sermon in the Book of Acts, longer even than Peter's at Pentecost. Stephen's sermon is an account of God's dealings with Israel through their holy history, a story well known to the council and to any faithful Jew. Stephen brought the sermon to its climax in a vigorous charge against the Jews, particularly in their crucifixion of Jesus. As he spoke the council members "began to grind their teeth" (7:54). Stephen now spoke still more forcefully. The council "battered him with stones" (7:59), even as Stephen prayed for their forgiveness as he died.

So it was that the first martyr and the preacher of the longest sermon was not one of the twelve, but a man chosen for a trusted but seemingly routine role, serving food to the widows. Stephen's speech also sparked a major persecution, so that the apostles were "scattered throughout the regions of Judea and Samaria" (8:1). Among those scattered was another table server, Philip. As he preached in Samaria, a revival broke forth so that "there was great rejoicing in that city" (8:8). The revival was of such proportions that the apostles commissioned Peter and John to go to Samaria to complete the work, so to speak.

Meanwhile, an angel directed Philip to "take the road that leads from Jerusalem to Gaza" (8:26), a desert road, where he encountered an Ethiopian official who was the chief financial officer in Queen Candace's government. A miraculous conversion and baptism followed, and this man carried the faith with him back to his homeland. Meanwhile, Philip continued "preaching the good news in all the cities until he reached Caesarea" (8:40).

Here's what I want us to see. The apostles had selected seven men to lead a delicate but rather routine administrative service, and almost immediately two of them take over the Acts story. Our chapter title raises the question, "Did the apostles make a mistake?" The apostles saw themselves as the ones especially assigned to prayer (and with it, miracles) and preaching, and saw their seven selected persons as able, anointed functionaries. I don't want to minimize the role of the seven, but I want us to recognize the difference in assignments. As the story unfolds, however, Stephen and Philip are more "apostolic" than most of the apostles.

Herein is the message of the Holy Spirit, of the Day of Pentecost, and of the church at its truest calling. As we noted earlier, in the Old Testament the Spirit of God came upon select persons—judges, kings, priests, and prophets. But in the New Testament, in the church, the Holy Spirit was poured out "on all people," sons and daughters, young and elders (2:17). Thus at Pentecost the witness to the Jerusalem crowds was not that of twelve apostles filled with the Spirit, but of 120—women and men, young and older—who were filled with the Spirit; and it was through these witnesses that people from everywhere heard "the mighty works of God in our own languages" (2:11).

Were the apostles mistaken in assuming that the grand work of ministry—prayer and preaching and general spiritual leadership—was theirs to do, and that the rest of the people were to take care of the more mundane tasks? And is it possible that the Holy Spirit was making clear that the apostolic perception was wrong, as demonstrated so forcefully by the work of Stephen and Philip? Consider that Stephen's sermon stands out in the Book of Acts, and that he was the first in "the noble company of martyrs"[1]; and ponder that Philip led the landmark revival in Samaria and by his witness and teaching sent the Gospel into Ethiopia. It's as if Philip were a one-person embodiment of Jesus' command that his followers carry the Gospel into "Samaria, and unto the uttermost parts of the earth" (1:8 KJV).

Of this I am sure: If the Day of Pentecost meant anything it was that the Holy Spirit was now the possession of all of God's people, not just a select group of leaders. And also this, that only rarely has the church allowed its lay persons to exercise fully their potential as God's Spirit-filled people.

There have been some magic moments along the way. The people who gathered around Francis of Assisi didn't pass through Holy Orders. By usual judgments, they must have seemed a sometimes motley crew. So, too, with the Lollards, who came into existence under the influence of John Wycliffe. Primarily, they were lay persons, and they survived continued persecution, laying the way for other movements of reform within the Catholic Church.

Martin Luther, the key figure of the Reformation, put the matter in theological terms in his teachings on the priesthood of all believers. "We are all alike Christians and have baptism, faith, the Spirit, and all things alike. If a priest is killed, a land is laid under an interdict. Why not in the case of a peasant? Whence comes this great distinction between those who are called Christians?"[2] Luther underlined this teaching when, in reducing the seven sacraments of Catholicism to just two, he eliminated the ordination of the clergy. He insisted that ordination was not a sacrament of the church but simply a rite by which a minister was empowered to discharge a particular office.

But it is one thing to declare a doctrine and quite another to live it out. Nor would I dare claim that my appeal for greater leadership from the laity is consonant with what Luther had in mind when he called for the priesthood of all believers. Nevertheless, Luther's bold statement has provided a frequent rallying cry in the church, and now and again new movements of lay leadership rise up, sometimes in a local congregation and sometimes in a full-scale movement.

The role of lay persons was basic in the eighteenth century Methodist movement in England. Although the founders of the movement, John and Charles Wesley, were ordained clergy of the Church of England, their converts were from the almost-forgotten laity in the church. Eventually, hundreds of those converts—miners, farmers, factory workers—became lay preachers. They studied books prepared by John Wesley specifically for their training. Some of them preached full-time, and others on weekends, to say nothing of the thousands who led small groups and did so in a way that was often both teaching and pastoral.

One of the most impressive lay movements in England is remembered as the Clapham Community, a loosely organized but profoundly dedicated group of well-to-do Englishmen led by William Wilberforce. They poured their lives into the private and public practice of their faith. History remembers them especially for their untiring battle to bring an end to slavery in England, but they were equally vigorous in dozens of other efforts on behalf of the poor, the sick, child laborers, and general practices of injustice. Wilberforce was himself a devout Methodist, but several of his closest friends in the Clapham Community were Calvinists.

The emphasis on the role of the laity in early Methodism carried over into its history in America in the nineteenth century. It was a natural fit for the frontier where often the ordained clergy could visit churches only once a month or less, and lay persons carried on in the meantime. Women came into roles of leadership in the holiness movement, with its roots in Methodism. The preeminent leaders in that movement were Phoebe Palmer, a Methodist, and Hannah Whitall Smith, a Quaker. They spoke widely in both America and England, and neither was ever ordained. Mrs. Palmer was a lay theologian to be reckoned with.

One of the most extraordinary revivals of religion in America occurred a few years before the Civil War in what is often called "the Businessmen's Revival." It was relatively short-lived, limited largely to a period in 1857–1858, but its impact was immense. Charles Finney, who knew something about revivals, estimated that fifty thousand conversions were occurring weekly across America.

It came at an unlikely time. The church, as well as the nation as a whole, was divided on the issue of slavery. Church membership was at a standstill. A New York businessman, Jeremiah Lanphier, began a noon prayer meeting on Wall Street. The first gathering was very small, and the second only a few persons larger. Within months, however, there were daily noontime prayer meetings in more than two thousand American cities, towns, and hamlets. It was a laymen's event (some women's groups sprang up in time), and most of the laymen were businessmen—perhaps primarily because only businessmen had the liberty of a full noon hour. Clergy were allowed to attend, but they didn't have positions of leadership. They were compelled, as were all participants in the services, to limit their witness to five minutes. Literature of the period notes that clergy were sometimes asked to sit down because they found it difficult to stay within the five-minute boundaries.

Students of American religious life estimate that this prayer meeting revival brought more souls into American churches in a short period than any revival before or since. It also saved the young YMCA movement—which at that time had a primarily religious emphasis—from extinction, and brought the American YWCA into existence. It also nurtured young Dwight L. Moody, the shoe salesman who became the best known evangelist in both America and England in the latter half of the nineteenth century and who was never ordained.

The twentieth and twenty-first centuries have seen a sprawling variety of Christian organizations started and led by lay persons. I rejoice in this, but I come back to the question of the chapter: Did the apostles make a mistake? I have purposely put the issue in an inflammatory way because I want us to see the profound issues that are involved. I won't challenge the apostles with a mistake, but I am impressed that the Holy Spirit seemed to rise above their action by the dramatic ministries of Stephen and Philip.

I'm very sure that if the church is to be what the Day of Pentecost ordained it to be we will see more leadership from farmers, business people, athletes, homemakers, attorneys, medical professionals, scientists, entrepreneurs—you name it!—who believe that their primary calling in life is not success or financial security, but service to God and humanity in the name and spirit of Christ. This is the essence, in the end, of the Holy Spirit coming not solely to religious professionals but to all of God's people.

6

Then There Was Paul

If you notice chapter titles you may have seen the similarity between chapter two and this chapter. It is intentional. As surely as the Day of Pentecost changed the little group of believers into the church, so the man first known to us as Saul of Tarsus, the man who cherished the title "apostle" though there were always those who would deny it to him, played the key role in what the church had become by the time the Book of Acts was written. He led the way in making the church an international body and gave the church the structure of doctrine that would save it from splintering into scores (probably hundreds) of meaningless sects. He is so crucial in the story of the early church and of all that follows that the second half of Acts belongs almost exclusively to him.

Some parts of Paul's story are as familiar to us as childhood Sunday school heroes like Joseph, Daniel, and David, but on others we're left to speculate. We know his city,

Tarsus, but we don't know the name of his mother and father, though they were clearly of more than ordinary standing. We know the name of his teacher, Gamaliel, and of his passion to be a Pharisee, but we don't know if he was ever married. Any Bible that has a section of maps will almost surely have several that document his travels, but we know him best for a road outside the city of Damascus where he was kept from fulfilling his appointment as a persecutor.

That roadway encounter is no doubt the most notable conversion story in Christian history. The stories of Jesus' first disciples are so economical in detail that you hardly know what happened: Jesus said, "Follow me," and they followed. Thousands were converted on the Day of Pentecost and in the weeks immediately following, but we have no details. Not so with Paul. He was on a mission of destruction, set on wiping out the followers of Jesus when he was stopped quite literally in his tracks.

The writer of Acts introduces Paul as a skilled modern movie maker might, focusing on him in a scene where of himself he seems to have no great significance. All eyes are on Stephen and his dramatic speech, then on the council members as they become a murdering mob. Then, "The witnesses placed their coats in the care of a young man named Saul" (Acts 7:58). A reader wonders who cares where the coats are laid. But before the paragraph ends, this further word, "Saul was in full agreement with Stephen's murder" (8:1). At this point the reader or the movie watcher mutters, "Keep your eyes on this 'young man.' "

We don't see him again, however, until after the exciting events with Philip, to which we referred in chapter five. By this time Saul seems to be leading the persecution of Jesus' followers. He is the emotional leader, if not the legally appointed one. "Meanwhile," the writer of Acts reports, "Saul was still spewing out murderous threats against the Lord's disciples" (9:1). He has gotten authorization from the high priest to seek out followers of the Way in Damascus, "whether men or women," so he can "take them as prisoners to Jerusalem" (9:2).

As Saul approaches Damascus, however, he is accosted by a friend of those he intends to arrest. A light from heaven encircles Saul, a light so powerful that he falls to the ground. Then, a voice from heaven addresses him personally, "Saul, Saul, why are you harassing me" (9:4). Saul knows that this is God, because he addresses him as "Lord" when he responds. The double call ("Saul, Saul") is familiar to Saul from his knowledge of the Hebrew Scriptures; this is the one who had called, "Moses, Moses," and "Samuel, Samuel." But how could this God Saul felt he knew so well, this God he was trying feverishly to serve, accuse him of harassing? The God Saul felt he knew should be endorsing his earnest mission. Imagine, then, when God answers, "I am Jesus, whom you are harassing" (9:5)! Saul had thought that in persecuting the followers of Jesus he was fulfilling the purposes of God. Instead, the God whom he adores is in truth the Jesus whom he has made the focal point of his murderous mission.

What follows seems anticlimactic, but it is essential to the highway accosting. Saul, blinded by the light, is taken by his companions to Damascus where he abstains from food and drink for three days in a house on Straight Street where a follower of the way, Ananias, comes to see him. Ananias knows of Saul's merciless mission, so he is reluctant to make such a visit. Nevertheless, when he comes to Saul's dwelling he greets him with one of the loveliest of greetings: "Brother Saul" (9:17). Saul has just been adopted into the family of the Way, by one of the persons whose life he was seeking when he came to Damascus.

Ananias explains that he has come because Jesus instructed him to do so, so that Saul could regain his sight and "be filled with the Holy Spirit. Instantly, flakes fell from Saul's eyes and he could see again. He got up and was baptized. After eating, he regained his strength" (9:17-19). For several days he remained in Damascus with unnamed disciples, but with no transition period and no orientation except for whatever conversations there may have been with these unnamed disciples. "Right away, he began to preach about Jesus in the synagogues. 'He is God's Son,' he declared" (9:20). This left his hearers "baffled" (9:21). And this was only the beginning.

Christian conversion is a glory and a miracle, whether it happens to Saul in a miraculous highway encounter or to those early believers in Jerusalem when "the Lord added daily to the community those who were being saved" (2:47). I love to read of conversions, whether it is the story of C. S. Lewis, whose conversion stretched over an extended period, or the story England's poet laureate, John Masefield, tells so gloriously in "The Everlasting Mercy." Charles Wesley wrote literally hundreds of hymns to rejoice in what conversion meant to him. I still remember the night, as a ten-year-old, when I went to a revival altar to ask Christ to save me. And the evening, shortly after high school graduation, when I knelt beside my best friend as he plowed through his intellectual questions to become a believer, and the evening I prayed alongside a Hollywood musician who was accompanist and arranger for some of the brightest stars of that era but who at that moment was seeking deliverance from his lostness in alcoholism. Or those scores of young people with whom I prayed at youth camps where I spoke often as a young preacher. I have never stopped marveling at conversions, whether simple or dramatic, a child or a hardened criminal, a grand worship service or a moment alone with God. Because, in the end, every transformed life is an eternal miracle.

Nevertheless, Paul's conversion was appropriate to the years that followed. He charged into Damascus to wipe out the followers of Jesus of Nazareth and before a week was out he was their most vigorous and compelling spokesman. It is high irony that he then ran into roadblocks from foes and friends alike. Some of his former associates plotted to kill him, but "his disciples" (there were already those who saw him as their leader) helped him to a nighttime escape by way of "a basket through an opening in the city wall" (9:25). But when he arrived in Jerusalem and tried to join the disciples there, "they were all afraid of him. They didn't believe he was really a disciple" (9:26).

The church at Jerusalem is a peculiar story. It deserves a book to itself, and no doubt several have written it. I'm troubled that so many—including the apostles—wanted to stay in Jerusalem, when Jesus had so clearly pointed beyond Jerusalem, to Judea, Samaria, and the uttermost parts of the world. I'm troubled that the time came when the new churches had to rescue them financially during a famine time. I'm troubled that they were so prone to institutionalism, which of course came easily when they were located in Judaism's historic city. And I'm troubled that they couldn't see the grace of God at work in Saul of Tarsus. They were a people for whom miracles were a daily menu. Surely they must have prayed for Saul's conversion. Yet when it came they were as dull to it as the night they were praying for Peter in his imprisonment, but when Rhoda the servant girl told them he was at the gate, they said she had lost her mind (12:5-15).

Paul's relationship to the Jerusalem church continued to be an uneasy one. Paul's Jewish heritage was such that he believed fully in organization, but he probably was better at directing than at following. All of us have our gifts, which is to say that we also have areas where we are not necessarily gifted. Paul's gifts were so many, so strong, and so forcefully demonstrated that they brought problems with them. He was hard to fence in. And of course he was so different from the original disciples. None of them came with credentials of scholarship, while Paul was a scholar through and through. They were mostly village men, at home primarily in the Jewish world. Paul was a city boy, a citizen of Tarsus (which he described as "an important city" [21:39]), who grew up in Jerusalem. Paul was passionately Jewish, but he was at home in the Gentile world, especially the world of Greek scholars. No doubt these differences between Paul and the Jerusalem leaders made them uneasy with him, and ready to be skeptical of his faith credentials.

Fortunately, there was one man in the Jerusalem leadership who believed in Paul's transformation. He was not a primary leader; that is, not one of the twelve. But his character and his devotion had won everyone's admiration and confidence. I'm speaking of the Levite from Cyprus, Barnabas. We'll return to him later. For now, note that when the leadership "didn't believe he was really a disciple....Barnabas brought Saul to the apostles and told them the story about how Saul saw the Lord on the way and that the Lord had spoken to Saul. He also told them about the confidence with which Saul had preached in the name of Jesus in Damascus" (9:26-27). As Luke reports the story one wonders if the leadership had even talked with Saul personally.

For a time he moved about freely, and spoke "with confidence in the name of the Lord" (9:28). Before long, however, Paul ran into opposition from some Greek-speaking Jews who set out to kill him. When Paul's fellow believers learned of this, they took him to Caesarea and "sent him off to Tarsus" (9:30).

We have no details about his time in Tarsus. There is no record of dynamic witnessing or making of converts. Certainly it was a private time in Paul's life and probably one of intense soul-searching. And with it, time to bring together several strands of knowledge. Paul was a scholar of the Hebrew Scriptures. Now he had time to ponder what he knew of Jesus with what he realized the prophets and psalmists had foreseen of him. Paul no doubt learned much of the teachings and personality of Jesus during the months when he was arresting and interrogating the people of the Way. Still more, during this period he received divine revelation, insight into the purposes of God that came to him through the Holy Spirit.

The time of essential isolation in Tarsus was not lost time. If Paul had continued the breakneck witnessing, debating, and converting that marked his first days as a convert in Damascus and the brief succeeding time in Jerusalem, one wonders if he would ever have had time to wait upon God's Spirit for the body of material that would later show itself in his letters to the churches. Paul was an activist. In later years he gloried in the miles of his journeys and his tireless activities. He needed the Tarsus interlude.

But the interlude, if I may call it that, was not an end. Again, there is Barnabas. Earlier, some of the believers who were driven from Jerusalem because of the persecution that followed Stephen's martyrdom went as far as Phoenicia, Cyprus, and Antioch. They preached only to Jews, but in the process reached many Jews who spoke only Greek. This presented a problem for the leadership in Jerusalem. They felt that someone with spiritual maturity should examine the situation in Antioch. They chose Barnabas, a great-hearted soul who was also a reliable scholar (a Levite, after all) and a man of judgment.

After a time in Antioch, while still more converts were coming in, "Barnabas went to Tarsus in search of Saul. When he found him, he brought him to Antioch" (11:25-26). The language suggests that the leaders in Jerusalem had lost contact with Saul. Barnabas became a detective on a mission. He searched until he found Saul. They then spent a year in Antioch, "meeting with the church and teaching large numbers of people" (11:26). The writer of Acts continues, "It was in Antioch where the disciples were first labeled 'Christians'" (11:26). Until then the believers were known as the "people of the Way." Now they were attached by name to their Lord and Savior.

Antioch was a thriving faith community. Acts tells us that the church there "included prophets and teachers" (13:1). Led by the Holy Spirit, the community laid hands on Barnabas and Saul and "sent them on their way...to Seleucia" (13:4). Then a change happened. The author tells us that Saul was also known as Paul. Then the team is described as "Paul and his companions" (13:13), as Paul begins to take the lead in miracle-working and in preaching. By general recognition the novice was becoming the senior partner.

After Paul and Barnabas returned to Jerusalem and prepared to set out on another missionary-evangelistic journey, a major difference arose between them. Barnabas's nephew (or in some translations, his cousin), John Mark, had deserted them on their previous journey, and when Barnabas urged that the young man rejoin them for the new journey, Paul disagreed. The issue became so intense that they went their separate ways, John Mark joining Barnabas as they headed to Cyprus, and Paul choosing Silas as they traveled through Syria and Cilicia.

From this point forward Paul steadily becomes the key personality in the story of the early church. Some will question his apostolic credentials to the end, perhaps "with jealous and competitive motives" (Philippians 1:15). Paul had known from his conversion that he was chosen to carry the name of Christ "before Gentiles, kings and Israelites"—and that in the process he "must suffer for the sake of my name" (Acts 9:15-16). It was he who carried the message into Europe, by way of a vision of "a man from Macedonia" (16:9). He was sure that it was his calling to plant churches and to go where others had not. It was he who boldly claimed that the church's message was "Christ crucified, which is a scandal to Jews and foolishness to Gentiles. But to those who are called—both Jews and Greeks—Christ is God's power and God's wisdom" (1 Corinthians 1:23-24).

He went by land and by sea. He suffered constant persecution, knowing that wherever he went he might be arrested and thrown in prison. He appeared before kings and varieties of authority, giving his testimony with such vigor that one potentate was sure that his much learning had made him insane. He was at home in a discussion on

Mars Hill, where "all Athenians as well as the foreigners who live in Athens used to spend their time doing nothing but talking about or listening to the newest thing" (Acts 17:21). But a majority of his work was with persons of whom it could be said that "not many were wise, not many were powerful, not many were from the upper class" (1 Corinthians 1:26).

But we know Paul best as a letter writer. In the history of literature, many have written more letters, many with an urbanity that Paul never sought and a cleverness that for him would have encumbered his message. But none wrote with greater passion, and no letter writer has begun to have his correspondence translated into more languages and dialects and quoted more widely. It was by those letters—written on the run, by dictation, often from prison cells—that he answered the questions of the first generation of believers, battled against the heresies that often threatened the faith, and established the doctrines that succeeding generations of church councils would confirm as the teachings of the church.

And he did it all as a pastor. Call him a missionary, an evangelist, a scholar, a theologian, a controversialist—he was all of these. But we will never understand him unless we recognize that above all he was a pastor, who wanted to confirm and encourage his fledgling believers so that they might know the fullness of life in Jesus Christ.

7

The Slow Process of Tumbling Walls

The early church had a problem that was slow of an answer. The problem has reappeared over the centuries, though in a variety of forms and styles. I can't give you a precise date of its first appearing, but I calculate it happened within the first year. And although the church was still very young, the problem itself had deep roots. In part, the issue was spiritual, and the ultimate integrity of the church eventually rested on how it was dealt with. But the spiritual issues were interwoven with some ancient ethnic prejudices that complicated matters still more because it is so easy for our secular prejudices to take on spiritual proportions. The basic issue was this: at the first, would the church be simply a branch of Judaism or would it be for all nations. And as the centuries unfold, will the church be especially for particular national, economic, or cultural groups, or equally open for all of God's people.

Here is the background. Virtually all of the first believers were Jewish or were converts to Judaism prior to their conversion to Christ. Judaism was by calling a witness to all nations. But by nature it was also exclusive. Indeed, if it lost its exclusivity, its calling was also in danger. Judaism dated its existence to the call of Abraham and Sarah. God had promised that they would become a "great nation," so significant that those who blessed them would be blessed and those who cursed them would be cursed. But this above all: "all the families of the earth will be blessed because of you" (Genesis 12:1-3). They would be the body of people through whom God's purposes would come to pass throughout the world.

If this were to happen, however, they would have to be a *holy* nation in order to represent a holy God. This meant living by some fundamental principles, such as the Ten Commandments, and also a variety of more detailed and specific rules of conduct, health, cleanliness, and even the food they ate. It included specific regulations forbidding or regulating marriage with other ethnic groups. Above all, there must be unique loyalty to the Lord God whom they served and who had called them to be a nation.

Over the centuries Judaism paid a high price for this calling. In those days every nation had its god or its panoply of gods, but Israel insisted that there was only one God and that they could serve no other. This invited persecution and being singled out as a peculiar people. Israel was not usually a national power except during the reigns of David and Solomon. Instead, their land was more often an area for other nations to pass through in the course of conquests. Nor did Israel find it easy to maintain their convictions. As we read the Old Testament prophets, we realize how often they compromised their standards and flirted with the practices of their pagan neighbors.

By the time the church was born, Judaism had been without a government of its own for most of six centuries. Many Jews had simply learned to exist in a Gentile world. Some had fully capitulated to the pagan cultures around them. The most devout, however, looked ever more earnestly for their Messiah, the Christ who would fulfill their calling as a nation.

Then came Jesus of Nazareth. He was not what many of them had expected, for though he spoke constantly of the Kingdom of God, he gave no sign of being a political leader. Instead he offered salvation, with a whole new way of life. Thus they were soon known as "the people of the Way"; then, because their salvation was in Jesus Christ, they began to be known as Christians.

The promise to Abraham included the idea of the whole world being blessed through his descendants, and Jesus was the expression of that "whole-world" blessing. John the Baptist identified him as "the Lamb of God who takes away the sin of the world" (John 1:29); not simply of one nation or ethnic group or even a confederation of nations, but a world without boundaries. So, too, with the grand, inclusive declaration: "God so loved the world that he gave his only Son, so that everyone who believes in him won't perish but will have eternal life" (3:16). The *world*.

Everyone who believes. Here was the ring of the promise given to Abraham: "all the families of the earth will be blessed because of you" (Genesis 12:3). No wonder, then, that Jesus told his followers that they would be his witnesses beginning in Jerusalem but going "to the end of the earth" (Acts 1:8).

This was magnificent language, and it was clear enough. But the early church soon learned that living it out was difficult. The Day of Pentecost was exciting: the message came through these 120 people in tongues that pilgrims to Jerusalem could understand, and they accepted it. But these were all Jews, and though so many of them now were more comfortable with the tongues of their adopted lands, still they were Jews. The fragility of the issue appears with the controversy over perceived inequities in distribution of food among the Greek-speaking and Aramaic-speaking widows in the Jerusalem congregation. It seemed such a minor matter, perhaps more an issue of perception than of fact; but our distinction between perception and fact so often rests on prior prejudices. Still, there's a definite sign of hope, not only in that the issue was resolved amicably but also that the seven chosen servers included "Nicolaus from Antioch, *a convert to Judaism*" (6:5; italics mine).

We see the Holy Spirit clearing the way in the early ministry of Philip. His revival in Samaria didn't call for any administrative action, but it surely shook ancient, angry prejudices because of the centuries-long hard feeling between the Jews and the Samaritans. As for the Ethiopian eunuch, no committee had an opportunity to vote on this matter because the Ethiopian asked if he could be baptized and Philip consulted no one before answering (colloquially), "Of course! Here's water. What else do we need?"

The issue took on entirely new dimensions, however, in the story of Cornelius, "a centurion in the Italian Company" (10:1). He was a remarkable man: "He and his whole household were pious, Gentile God-worshippers. He gave generously to those in need among the Jewish people and prayed to God constantly" (10:2). It's hard to beat those credentials. Except, of course, that the man is a Gentile. And no doubt, for others, a military man, which for Jews carried a stigma of Roman oppression.

There are two other actors in this story: the apostle Peter and the Holy Spirit. For a Catholic reader, Peter is significant indeed, since he is seen as the first leader of the church, but for any generation including his own, Peter was the sort of person who would be wherever the lightning struck. Sometimes we think this is because Peter is so quick to speak up. But perhaps it's also because he is open to the touch of the Holy Spirit. He may not always speak with considered precision, but he is quick to hear.

The Holy Spirit spoke to both men by way of visions. Both men received orders. For Cornelius the orders were brief: God had seen his good heart. He should send messengers to find one "known as Peter" (10:5), and bring him to Cornelius's home. Peter's vision was longer, partly because he wasn't a military person like Cornelius and not as accustomed to accepting orders as given, and partly because for him it was going to be a much more complicated matter. Cornelius wouldn't mind having Peter in his home, but Peter wasn't naturally inclined to go there.

Peter's vision included a dramatic event. The message was sharp: "Never consider unclean what God has made pure" (10:15). While Peter was still brooding over the meaning of his vision, Cornelius's representatives arrived with their invitation, and the Holy Spirit advises Peter, "Don't ask questions; just go with them because I have sent them" (10:20). Peter received the men into his house as guests: a huge step for an observant first-century Jew.

What follows the next day is beautiful and heart-warming. The Holy Spirit, the Lord of Pentecost for all peoples and tongues, is at work. Peter takes with him "some of the believers from Joppa" (10:23). Cornelius gathers both "relatives and close friends" (10:24). The two men give their respective testimonies as to what the Spirit of God has done in their lives. Peter has had another conversion: "I really am learning that God doesn't show partiality to one group of people over another. Rather, in every nation, whoever worships him and does what is right is acceptable to him" (10:34-35).

Peter then seeks to give a synopsis of the Gospel. He has just gotten to the point of forgiveness of sins through the nation of Jesus when "the Holy Spirit fell on everyone who heard the word. The circumcised believers who had come with Peter were astonished that the gift of the Holy Spirit had been poured out even on the Gentiles. They heard them speaking in other languages and praising God" (10:44-46). As always, Peter is a man of action.

" 'These people have received the Holy Spirit just as we have. Surely no one can stop them from being baptized with water, can they' " (10:47). They baptized them in the name of Jesus Christ, and Cornelius invited Peter to "stay for several days" (10:48). I suspect those days were a short course in faith and belief.

But now, it was institution time! How would the apostolic leadership in Jerusalem respond to Peter's story? No one was better equipped to be the point man than Peter. Others might be better logicians, but Peter (with James and John) was part of the trio that had been closest to Jesus. He was the one who had declared of Jesus, "You are the Christ, the Son of the living God," and it was of his statement that Jesus had said, "I'll build my church on this rock" (Matthew 16:16, 18).

The news of Peter's time with Cornelius got to Jerusalem before he did, and when he appeared, "the circumcised believers criticized him. They accused him, 'You went into the home of the uncircumcised and ate with them' " (Acts 11:2-3). Even Peter's standing was not enough to justify his violation of the traditional barrier between Jew and Gentile. The people at Jerusalem had heard that these uncircumcised Gentiles had been filled with the Holy Spirit, just as they had been on the Day of Pentecost, but still they couldn't accept that Peter would eat with such outsiders. The wall of separation was high, deep, and apparently impregnable.

So Peter set out, "step-by-step" (11:4), to tell what had happened. As we read the story, nearly twenty centuries later, we can still sense the intensity of feelings. I remember a historian who said of a particular European ethnic group, "They think with their blood!" Such was surely the case that day with the leadership in Jerusalem. They were thinking, not reasonably and certainly not charitably; they were thinking with their blood. Peter concluded his report just as he had settled the matter in his own mind several days earlier: "If God gave them the same gift he gave us who believed in the Lord Jesus Christ, then who am I? Could I stand in God's way" (11:17)? With this, the group "calmed down. They praised God and concluded, 'So then God has enabled Gentiles to change their hearts and lives so that they might have new life' "(11:18).

But it was not the end. Walls that have existed for centuries, that seem to bear God's imprimatur, and that satisfy one's own ethnic sense of specialness are not going to disappear that easily and completely. But the Holy Spirit doesn't stay within the walls we humans raise up. When Paul and Barnabas returned to Antioch, where they had enjoyed successful ministry, they noted "how God had opened a door of faith for the Gentiles" (14:27). The writer of Acts hasn't prepared us for this sentence, nor does he enlarge upon it. We conclude that the grace that was at work in Greek-speaking Jews and also in Gentiles who had converted to Judaism (as with Cornelius) was now drawing in more and more Gentiles—uncircumcised and with no background in Judaism. Barnabas and Paul, being men of faith, recognized that God had opened the door of faith and the Gentiles were coming in.

Some Christian legalists saw it, too, and they were not glad. They told these new converts that unless they also accepted the teachings of Moses—particularly circumcision—they couldn't be saved (15:1). So the church at Antioch sent Paul, Barnabas, "and several others" to go to Jerusalem and present the question "before the apostles and the elders" (15:2). The group traveled through Phoenicia and Samaria, "telling stories about the conversion of the Gentiles to everyone. Their reports thrilled the brothers and sisters" (15:3). The conversions that were bringing fear and apprehension to the legalists were bringing joy to many others.

The Jerusalem leaders met the issue head on. When the Antioch delegation reported what was happening, a group of believers "from among the Pharisees" countered that Gentiles "'must be required to keep the Law from Moses'" (15:5).

It was a crucial hour in the life of the infant church. After extended debate, Peter rose to speak. He not only referred to his personal experience, he reasoned with his fellow leaders. He said that God, who knows our humanity's "deepest thoughts and desires" (15:8) had purified the deepest thoughts and desires of Gentiles through faith. When God has seen fit to do this, how dare we challenge God by placing a burden on their shoulders that "neither we nor our ancestors could bear?" Peter insisted that these Gentiles were "saved in the same way, by the grace of the Lord Jesus" (15:9-11). It was a powerful statement. Then Barnabas and Paul described the "signs and wonders God did among the Gentiles" (15:12) through their ministry. Then James, the brother of Jesus, quoted the prophet Amos to support what had been said.

The official body prepared a letter to go out to the churches. Here are the essentials, they said: "refuse food offered to idols, blood, the meat from strangled animals, and sexual immorality" (15:29).

This may seem to us a strange combination: food offered to idols, blood, the meat from strangled animals, and sexual immorality. When Gentiles offered meat sacrifices in their pagan worship, part was given to the gods and the rest was taken by worshipers for their own use, especially for social feasting. For believers to eat such food involved them in the worship of the false gods. Blood itself was an issue at the heart of Hebrew worship, because blood represented life; thus blood was always treated sacredly. This principle carried over into Christianity in the teaching that we are saved by the blood of Christ. We celebrate this conviction each time we receive the sacrament of Holy Communion, when we say, as we raise the cup, "The blood of Christ, given for you." These rules are not as remote as at first they seem, especially if we are properly sensitive to the power of symbols and rituals.

The issue of "sexual immorality" should be easy for us to grasp. Perhaps there was no time in social history when sexual immorality was more prevalent and more accepted than in the first-century world. William Barclay reminds us that some feel that "chastity was the only completely new virtue that Christianity brought into the world."[1]

Intervening generations may not have dealt with sexual immorality at the level of the first century until our own time.

The message was delivered in written form by two of the most respected leaders in the church, Judas and Silas. As they delivered the word, "they said many things that encouraged and strengthened the brothers and sisters" (15:32), and they stayed long enough to be a pastoral presence and not just delegates from church headquarters.

Prejudices and deep convictions don't die easily, however. We know from Paul's Letter to the Galatians that there continued to be those in the church who insisted that Gentile believers ought also to be circumcised before being fully accepted as Christians. Paul was emphatic: "if we become righteous through the Law, then Christ died for no purpose" (Galatians 2:21).

The first generation of believers had to deal with centuries of ethnic barriers. The walls were slow to tumble down. We can admire our spiritual ancestors for dealing with this very human but very spiritual issue so charitably but with such certain conviction. Beliefs matter, because beliefs determine conduct. A church without doctrine is a self-contradiction. The problem for the church is to maintain the basics without which it is meaningless, but to do so with charity and compassion.

8

The Man Who Saved the New Testament

Yes, my title is overly dramatic. I'm sure we would have a New Testament today if there had not been the man Joseph of Cyprus, wonderfully nicknamed Barnabas, because the church itself would not have survived without its basic document. As it happened, however, Barnabas was the person of destiny. He was the right person at the right times and in the right places; and especially, he was a person who was ready to be used by God.

We've already met Barnabas, but let me remind us of what we already know while adding some pertinent details. He was a man with special credentials, in that he belonged to the tribe of Levi. The Levites were Israel's priestly tribe, meaning that they not only led worship, they were also the nation's legal authorities, their musicians, and their teachers. They were no more free of sin and error than their fellow Israelites, but they carried great ancestral responsibility.

He was a native of Cyprus. This meant that if he were to fulfill some of the more prestigious roles of his priesthood, he had to journey to Jerusalem to do so. His parents named him Joseph, which was of course an honored and popular name among the Jews. The name didn't capture the particular character of the man, however, so his fellow believers chose to call him *Barnabas*. The writer of Acts makes clear the significance of the name at its first mentioning: *one who encourages* (Acts 4:36, italics mine). As his story unfolds we will see how right the apostles were in their nickname and how beautifully Barnabas lived up to it.

We first meet him in a story of his generosity: he sold a field and brought the money to the apostles for them to use as they saw fit. In truth, he was one of scores or perhaps hundreds who did such a thing at that time in the life of the church. Perhaps the size of his gift drew special attention, and perhaps also because apparently it was his gift—unfortunately!—that led to the deception by Ananias and Sapphira. More important, however, is that this gift was so typical of Barnabas's whole personality.

We next read of Barnabas when the church needed a special person for a delicate task. The Holy Spirit's activity in Antioch was beyond the expectations of the apostles, and they wanted to be sure that everything happening there was appropriate. So they sent Barnabas to Antioch to do a study. Here's how Luke reports it: "When he arrived and saw evidence of God's grace, he was overjoyed and encouraged everyone to remain fully committed to the Lord." Then Luke adds what we might call an editorial comment. "Barnabas responded in this way because he was a good man, whom the Holy Spirit had endowed with exceptional faith" (11:23-24).

Notice the way Barnabas responded to the situation in Antioch. He was there under assignment to evaluate what was happening. The leaders in Jerusalem were cautious; they had the good sense to know that their young movement was susceptible to all kinds of problems. I think they also recognized that while enthusiasm is powerful, it can also be dangerous. Barnabas was an intelligent man; they could trust him to know the difference between excitement and reality.

But especially, Barnabas was a deeply spiritual man. When he saw the grace of God at work, "he was overjoyed." He knew when to stop critiquing and to begin encouraging. Luke, the author of Acts, gives a simple phrase, but all the more powerful because of its simplicity: Barnabas was a *good* man. He belonged to a religious community where goodness was the norm, and in the midst of such goodness, his goodness stood out. Then, this: that the Holy Spirit had "endowed him with exceptional faith." Again, this: faith was the norm in this community. They were all persons of faith. But the faith of Barnabas was *exceptional*. I think of Jesus' parable of the man who was looking for a pearl of great price, one of a kind. He shopped in places where pearls were in trade, and in the midst of hundreds of pearls, one stood out. So it was with Barnabas. In a community where everyone was good, Barnabas was a pearl that stood out. In a body where faith was a standard commodity, possessed by all, Barnabas was a wealthy man, so to speak.

Most of all, he was an *encourager*. If he erred, it was on the side of hope and goodness. He saw more goodness than did even the typical saint. He *liked* goodness, so he saw it where others did not. Some people seem naturally to gravitate toward pessimism. Barnabas gravitated toward hope. He looked for the best and he saw the best—often where others simply couldn't. Perhaps that's the difference between faith and exceptional faith. In some settings, almost anyone can have faith; the person of exceptional faith believes when the evidence is hard to come by.

A key factor in goodness is humility. Humility is not shown by self-despising. Indeed, humility is a complex grace of many parts. But among other things, humility has the ability to recognize and rejoice in the quality of others. Those who are self-absorbed rarely recognize the gifts possessed by others or, doing so, resent them. When Barnabas saw the good thing that was happening in Antioch, he knew that it should be tended by someone whose teaching and leadership could bring out the best. He thought of Saul of Tarsus. As I indicated earlier, Saul seems almost to have dropped from the scene. He was somewhere back in Tarsus. Barnabas set out to find him. And he didn't trust the search to anyone else.

What did Barnabas know about Saul that the other leadership did not? Perhaps he reasoned that Saul, like himself a Jew who had lived in the Gentile world, was better equipped to understand the people who were coming into the Antioch church. Perhaps he saw that Saul, as a relatively new convert, would have increased empathy for these new believers. Perhaps he was impressed by the clarity of Saul's mind and his ability to put his thoughts in vigorous idioms and metaphors and to do so with a passion uncommon in a scholar of such depth.

If so, how is it that others didn't see these things in Saul? I think it comes around to the three words that the author of Acts uses in describing Barnabas. He was a *good* man, we're told. This suggests that Barnabas saw goodness where others saw potential trouble. Every human package should be marked, "Handle with care," because each person has a share of good and ill. The proportions differ markedly; some people are an almost unceasing delight to work with while others test the patience of all their teammates. Barnabas saw persons through the lens of goodness; for him their virtues were enlarged and their irritants minimized.

And he was an *encourager*. He hated to see others lose; he wanted people to succeed. What others might throw on the scrap heap, Barnabas thought needed only some loving dusting and polishing. Barnabas was the kind of teacher who, instead of giving a student a failing grade, writes a note: "You have some problems, but I think we can solve them."

This quality of encouragement was augmented by the other word the writer of Acts uses in explaining Barnabas: he had *exceptional faith*. There's a spiritual quality in

Barnabas that is more than simply a personality trait. The Bible lists nine qualities as the "fruit of the Spirit" (Galatians 5:22). All of them are traits that exist in our common secular culture; they aren't unique to the church or to Christians. But the biblical writer wants us to know that the Holy Spirit endows some persons with these qualities in a larger-than-human size. There is love; every person knows something about love. But then there is love that is a step beyond human understanding—a fruit of the Spirit. So with joy, and peace, and faith. Barnabas had *exceptional* faith. He employed this faith redemptively in human beings. Gal 5 : 22-23

So Barnabas sought out Saul when it seems that the general church leadership had forgotten him. And he put him to work, as a teammate. The language of Acts is, as you may have noticed, revealing. At first we read of "Barnabas and Saul" (Acts 13:2, 7). Then we're told that Saul was also known as Paul (13:9), and we see him in a dramatic leadership moment. Next the writer refers to "Paul and his companions" (13:13), and Paul is the spokesman in a lengthy sermon excerpt, after which it is "Paul and Barnabas" (13:50-51; 14:1) until they report to the Jerusalem assembly, where Barnabas is still the esteemed figure and he is mentioned first (15:12). In the world of business we would say that Barnabas invited Saul to join his firm and shortly thereafter Saul became the managing partner and president.

There is no hint that this development upset Barnabas. He was a *good* man and big enough that he took life in

stride. But a test was just ahead. After a time Paul suggested
that the two of them visit cities where they had preached,
to see how the churches were doing. Barnabas liked the
idea, and suggested that they take John Mark (Barnabas's
nephew) with them. He had been with them during part
of their previous journey but had left them at Pamphylia
(13:13), returning home to Jerusalem. Paul was unhappy
with John Mark's departure, feeling that the young man
had forsaken them. Barnabas insisted that they give him
another chance. Luke puts the point succinctly: "Their
argument became so intense that they went their separate
ways" (15:39). Paul took Silas and with the blessing of
the church "traveled through Syria and Cilicia, strengthening the churches." Barnabas took Mark and sailed to his
homeland on the island of Cyprus (15:39-41).

What shall we say about this vigorous disagreement
between two premier personalities in the early church—
the one especially praised for his goodness and the other
notable for his impassioned leadership as missionary, evangelist, scholar, and pastor? Who was right?

In my judgment, both were right. But they were different personalities, reasoning from different vantage points
and working with different expectations. Paul saw a young
man who had forsaken his colleagues; Barnabas saw a
young man (and yes, one who happened also to be his
nephew) who did the kind of foolish thing that the young
(and sometimes the older) are likely to do. Paul saw a boy
who needed to grow up; Barnabas saw one he intended to
help grow up. Paul saw the kingdom, and the dedication

necessary to do kingdom work; Barnabas saw a person who in time would be valuable to the kingdom. As a result of their disagreement, Paul became mentor to Silas and a host of others, and Barnabas did his particular work of encouragement, with much of the investment in John Mark. More of that later!

The reference to Barnabas and John Mark going to Cyprus is the last mention of Barnabas in the Book of Acts. He seems to drop out of the story at this point. He reappears, however, in three of Paul's letters. In his first letter to the church at Corinth Paul refers to himself and Barnabas as among the few who supported themselves rather than depending on offerings from the churches; this is obviously an affectionate reference. In the second chapter of Galatians Paul recites something of the struggle to open the church to Gentiles, and the part he and Barnabas played in that drama. Paul notes that the pressure became so great that "even Barnabas got carried away with" the others "in their hypocrisy" (Galatians 2:13). This is a tribute in its own way to Paul's high expectations for Barnabas. In writing to the Colossians, Paul refers to Mark as "Barnabas' cousin," urging the people at Colossae "if he [Mark] comes to you, welcome him" (Colossians 4:10).

Obviously Paul now sees Mark's value. But he makes the point still more emphatically in his Second Letter to Timothy. Paul is writing from prison and feeling his aloneness. Demas, who had been one of his young associates, has forsaken him because he has "fallen in love with the present world." Other young associates, Crescens and

Titus, are on distant assignments. "Only Luke is with me." Paul appeals, "Get Mark, and bring him with you. He has been a big help to me in the ministry" (2 Timothy 4:9-11). A New Testament scholar of another generation translated Paul's words this way: "Bring Mark, for he can turn his hand to anything."[1] Paul makes no reference to John Mark's earlier failure. Perhaps he's forgotten it. Perhaps he'd rather not remind himself of his harsh judgment at that earlier time. Whatever, John Mark has more than justified Barnabas's unceasing belief in him.

Many of us can remember a teacher, a parent, or a friend who believed in us when there was limited reason to do so. Some of us look back on such a person as a turning point in life. "Where would I be today," we ask, "if it weren't for her, for him?" There is no proving such a matter beyond argument; someone can always answer that another person or a later development could have worked the same redemptive wonder. Still, I wonder. Those persons who dare to see our worth when the general populace votes otherwise, those who stand alongside when the road is very lonely; those, that is, who are God's encouragers, are a history-shaping breed. Indeed, an eternity-shaping breed. When we read that Barnabas had exceptional faith, consider that it was a faith in God that showed itself by its faith in persons. Faith in God is sometimes rather intangible. Faith in persons comes in the grit and struggle of life, and we show it by the way we respond to persons, particularly in times of trouble or when others are rejecting that person.

I think it's clear that Barnabas was an extraordinarily fine person. It's easy to see why his fellow believers held him in such high esteem. Most of us wish we had a Barnabas on our side, "covering our back," as the contemporary phrase puts it. But what does this have to do with the extravagant title of this chapter, "The Man Who Saved the New Testament"?

Look first at Paul. For centuries he has been known as the author of thirteen New Testament letters. Some modern scholarship reasons that several of these letters were written by students or colleagues of Paul, who were either writing on Paul's behalf or who intended to express Paul's convictions. Even if one holds to this position, however, the epistles in question still are related to Paul. These letters not only occupy a substantial part of the New Testament, they are the source and structure of the basic body of Christian doctrine and ethics. Paul's counsel ranges all the way from the nature of Christ and God's plan for the universe to daily conduct in the world of work, marriage, running of the church, our relationship to government, and our daily moral code—to mention only a few! It is clear that no one in the first century of believers was equipped to do what Paul did. Hundreds, indeed, thousands, could teach, preach, evangelize, and begin and establish churches, but no one else had Paul's gift for speaking to Jews and Gentiles, and to shopkeepers and philosophers, and to write effectively.

The best evidence of this, of course, is in the way his letters survived. They got their hearing by sheer quality, not by the action of any church body; that came later. I like to say that they survived by the democracy of the Holy Spirit. Those early believers copied Paul's letters by hand, often at the peril of their relationships and of life itself because they believed that what they were saving was from God. I concur with their conviction.

So it is that I ask myself if there would have been Paul, the supreme letter-writer/theologian, if it hadn't been for Barnabas. Would Paul have been lost somewhere in Tarsus, never coming to his full ministry?

Then there's John Mark. Tradition knows him as the author of the second Gospel—the Gospel most scholars feel was the first written. Would there have been a John Mark to give us this dynamic picture of our Lord if it hadn't been for the day Barnabas broke with Paul and insisted on giving the young man a second chance?

I know, I know: God is bigger than Barnabas or any other passing human servant. Nevertheless, honor should be paid to those whom God uses. In my judgment, Barnabas is one of God's key persons.

I suspect that Barnabas erred in some reclamation projects that we know nothing about. That's the price of being an encourager: you don't always win. For me, however, no New Testament person other than our Lord is so worthy of admiration than this man who was *good* and possessed of *exceptional faith*. Faith in God and in people. And that made an eternal difference.

9

The Anonymous Apostles

W e noted at the beginning of our study that the late J. B. Phillips said that if we translated the title of Acts literally it would be "Acts of Apostles," or more clearly, "Some Acts of Some Apostles." It's time we talked about the unnamed apostles.

I am using the word *apostle* in a controversial way, I'm doing so purposely, yet I don't really want my usage to get in the way of my point. I do want, however, to underline the extraordinary role of a great number of unknown or relatively unknown persons.

We generally think of there being only twelve apostles— the original body of disciples, with Matthias later taking the place of Judas. There are good reasons for this position. One of the most interesting is in the Book of Revelation. As that book nears its dramatic close it describes the Holy City as being built on twelve foundations, and those foundations bear the names of the twelve apostles of the Lamb

(Revelation 21:14). Whether Revelation uses the word *apostle* symbolically or literally, it surely makes clear that it's not a word to use casually.

But as important as these twelve men were, the Book of Acts tells us very little about their specific roles in the first generation of the church. Peter became the spokesperson and a very courageous and persuasive one on the Day of Pentecost. Soon thereafter he and John were key in a miracle of healing that seemed to declare that, as Jesus had said, the works that he had done his followers would do, and "even greater works than these" (John 14:12). James, however, was martyred rather early, and although Peter played a key role in the admitting of Gentiles into the church we read little of him in the second half of Acts. As for the other nine apostles, we read nothing, although we assume they were part of the ruling council to whom all major questions were brought.

Jesus' great commission, that his followers should take the message into all the world, was given first to the eleven (before Matthias was chosen to succeed Judas), yet it seems in Acts that they stayed rather much in Jerusalem. Tradition and legend, however, have them going "into all the world." Such traditions and legends are not the point of this book; our interest here is with the confirmed material in Acts. Nevertheless, it's worth looking at these reports for a moment. At the least these traditions and legends have some measure of foundation in fact.

Start with Peter. We think of him primarily for his presence in Rome and his eventual leadership there. His brother Andrew is credited with far wider travels; he is revered as the patron saint of Russia, Greece, and Scotland because he is said to have ministered in all of those countries. Tradition says that Philip ministered in Asia, with martyrdom in Hierapolis. Simon the Zealot is remembered as evangelizing in Persia and in the British Isles.

Many of us might have a hard time remembering Nathanael as one of the twelve, but he has his place in tradition and legend for preaching in Phrygia, India, and Armenia. Matthew is related to Ethiopia, Persia, and Macedonia, and Thaddeus to Persia and Armenia. Thomas's place is permanently set by his name; the ancient church in India is still known as the Mar Thoma Church, the only body of Christendom bearing the name of an apostle. You'll find a Mar Thoma Church in Greater Chicago. Thaddeus, another of the lesser-known apostles, is said to have preached in Persia and Armenia. And Matthias, who came into the twelve late as the substitute for Judas, has roots in Arabia, Ethiopia, and areas bordering both the Red Sea and the Black Sea. None of these traditions, however, are substantiated in the Book of Acts.

Our interest in this chapter, however, goes far beyond the twelve, and beyond the apostle Paul, who dominates so much of Acts. Yes, and beyond such great souls as Barnabas, who was so crucial to Paul, and to people associated later with Paul, like Silas, Timothy, Titus, and Priscilla and Aquila, to name a few. I'm thinking of persons known to us only by some identifying reference in some particular occasion or by their association with some better known figure. Still more, I include in this "anonymous" group, persons who really are unknown to us, thoroughly anonymous, yet whose work is surely inferred in the Book of Acts.

In calling them "apostles" I'm using the term carefully and reverently, but more broadly. Professor Craig Keener tells us that in the first century, *apostle* meant literally someone who was a messenger commissioned to carry out the sender's mission, and that in the New Testament the term applied to those "agents of Christ authorized in a special way (more authoritatively than others) to declare and propagate his will."[1] Paul saw himself as such an apostle, though he was not one of the original twelve. I don't know how many persons like himself—that is, believers who never saw Jesus in the flesh—Paul would have included with himself in the sacred term. In truth, probably not many, if any, because Paul had a very high estimate of the office of an apostle.

So I'm stretching the matter. I have a larger, different company in mind. Almost all in my group seem inconspicuous to the point of unimportance, partly because they would number in the hundreds and perhaps even in the thousands: people who saw themselves serving Christ wherever they might be but whose names and specific actions are rarely if ever mentioned. I'm quite sure these persons would be surprised to hear that centuries later some writer would give them the apostolic title. I do so because the Book of Acts and the church it describes would be unimaginable without these people, whatever title one gives them. And I dare to use the apostolic term to indicate my regard for these persons and to highlight their importance in establishing the early church. And yes, to indicate my belief that the ultimate wonder of the church rests so heavily upon such persons, even if their names are generally unknown beyond the small body who know them best (perhaps even while taking them for granted).

I think for instance of a supporting character in the story of Cornelius, the centurion in the Italian company who was a Gentile God-worshipper and the first such person to come into the church. When an angel instructed Cornelius to send messengers to Simon Peter, Cornelius summoned two of his household servants "along with a pious soldier from his personal staff" (Acts 10:7). We don't know this soldier's name. We never hear of him again. But the author of Acts has told us enough to make us realize that this man was important in the faith life of Cornelius and a key figure in Cornelius's story.

Beyond doubt this "pious soldier" was a spiritual confidante to Cornelius. In the tough, often crude world of professional soldiers there was little time for religion— just as is sometimes the case in our contemporary world of finance, law, advertising, entertainment, or journalism. Such daily occupations become all-consuming, and when some elements of the occupation are made morally marginal by circumstances, it's all the more a lonely road for a person of faith. Cornelius knew that this "pious soldier" would know how to relate to Simon Peter, that they would have an instinctive bond in the Spirit. I can't imagine the Cornelius story without him. I wonder what happened to him later. Was his family among the first in Rome or some other Italian city to become followers of Christ? Did he become a leader in some local house church or in a company of soldiers who became believers? Did he help establish churches wherever the Roman military sent him? I wish I knew his story!

And think of those persons who experienced miracles. Consider the man who was asking alms from Peter and John at the gate of the temple, who instead was quite wonderfully healed. Or the young woman in Philippi who was being exploited as a psychic until Paul delivered her. Or the numbers of persons who sent items to Paul for his anointing so that they might be healed (19:11-12), or those who brought their sick where the shadow of Peter might bring healing as he passed by (5:15-16). What was the power of testimony in the persons who were converted or who saw the difference that happened to family members or friends who were converted? How many of them felt compelled to tell others what they had seen and experienced? How many of them took their new faith to the next town, where they had friends and relatives?

I think, too, of persons to whom Acts makes a sweeping reference early in the story: "Even a large group of priests embraced the faith" (6:7). Here were men who carried the authority of their Levitical office. They were scholars, held in reverence by the people, trained in the faith of Israel. Acts gives us no further report of any of these persons, yet no doubt many of them became part of what Paul later refers to as prophets, evangelists, pastors, and teachers (Ephesians 4:11). What was the gracious fall-out of their new faith? It's hard to imagine that some of those persons with such background and standing didn't become missionaries, teachers, and pastors in the growing body of believers.

I confess that I have no statistics to offer, and most of the persons in my formula are, as I've indicated, anonymous. But nothing is so contagious as a thoroughly convinced convert. We need to keep in mind that while the church had a structure for dealing with doctrinal issues in the Jerusalem apostolic body, the rest of the organization was relatively flexible. There was not yet a system that determined who should be ordained or licensed and who not; people were accepted for the spiritual gifts they possessed.

This kind of structure, or lack thereof, sounds strange to our culture, where denominations have stated requirements for ordination and leadership, usually with a prescribed number of years of education and preparatory experience. But whether for good or ill, we're not unacquainted with what I'm describing. The growth of charismatic Christian bodies, especially in the southern hemisphere, gains much of its strength from just such persons. They are often limited in organized training but strong in zeal, dedication, and faith. There's a holy contagion in such persons. They need a Peter, a Paul, or a John to answer their questions, but the daily world around them needs their witness.

Early Methodism, in both the British Isles and America, depended heavily on such persons. At first John Wesley, Oxford scholar that he was, was cautious about using such earnest but untrained converts. Certainly he found it hard to imagine them in places similar to the conventional offices of the Anglican church. But his mother, Susanna, convinced him that these persons could be as truly called of God as he was. So Wesley set about training such persons. In some instances this meant to begin by teaching them to read, but always it was with a command to study, and Wesley provided the books they would use. They didn't have the classical education of Oxford or Cambridge, but they gave their whole persons to prayer and study, and if they weren't ready to devote themselves to such study Wesley quickly disabused them of any idea of calling. In truth, they had something of an advantage over professional scholars because in their life experience they were so close to the people to whom they ministered. I believe it was the late Roy L. Smith who said, "The person who has an experience with God has something beyond the reach of any argument." This surely was the mood of the first generation of believers, and it has reasserted itself in each period of renewal within the church.

But what was the early secret of such steady growth? Sometimes it was spectacular, as in the early days in Jerusalem, then in Samaria and Antioch. But more often, I'm sure, it was the "ordinary" growth that came through the work of forgotten persons. There were persons whose name is in the record but still nearly anonymous: like

Mnason, who provided lodging for Paul and his friends when they were in Jerusalem: "He was from Cyprus and had been a disciple a long time" (21:16). What shall we say for those persons who are followers "a long time," providing lodging when needed, often filling a gap unnoticed. We know of the evangelist Philip, who was so significant early in the story, in Samaria and then to the Ethiopian eunuch; but what of his "four unmarried daughters who were involved in the work of prophecy" (21:9)? In a world where most public address was left to men, here were four women gifted to speak in public, who must have given great heart to other women whose lives were touched by the Spirit.

And when we read of the early revival at Antioch under Paul and Barnabas, the writer of Acts tells us that they did their work "together with many others [as] they taught and proclaimed the good news of the Lord's word" (15:35). Who were these "many others"? Soon after Paul and Silas teamed up to visit the churches, they "traveled through Syria and Cilicia, strengthening the churches" (15:41). Who started those churches and who sustained them between notable visitors like Paul? Paul writes later to the people at Corinth of the way God's work prospered, "I planted, Apollos watered, but God made it grow" (1Corinthians 3:6). For every church that Paul planted and Apollos watered, I wonder how many were planted by unknown persons, then watered by persons even less known? Only God's act of growth was the same.

I ask myself where all of the early churches came from. Who did it? Paul and his team "traveled from place to place in the region of Galatia and the district of Phrygia, strengthening all the disciples" (18:23). Who started all of those churches? When Paul "wanted to travel to Achaia, the brothers and sisters encouraged him and wrote to the disciples so they would open their homes to him" (18:27). Obviously Paul was not at that time a familiar figure in Achaia; who planted the churches there? Later, when Paul and his team arrived in Ptolemais, they "greeted the brothers and sisters there and spent a day with them" (21:7). Who started the church at Ptolemais? This is the only reference to it in the Book of Acts. Obviously some courageous soul found his or her way there. And when Paul is nearing the end of his journey, as recorded in Acts, they left their ship for a day in Puteoli. "There," Luke tells us, "we found brothers and sisters who urged us to stay with them for a week" (28:14). Again, this is all we know about Puteoli. How is it that there were believers there, ready to extend hospitality to Paul? Who planted the church at Puteoli? Corinth we know, Thessalonica we know, so too with Antioch and Samaria, Ephesus and Rome; but who is the story behind Ptolemais and Puteoli, Phrygia and some churches in Cilicia?

I find something wonderfully symbolic in the vision Paul received when the Holy Spirit instructed him to move into Europe. It was a "man from Macedonia" (16:9). Not a businessman, a farmer, or a teacher—just a *man*. Altogether anonymous, with no qualifying authority or credentials, who somehow represented the whole needy human race located in that huge territory. And it is more than a little significant that the first named convert there was a woman, Lydia, who had been seeking for God with no specific, named reason. And when Paul and his team left that early European outpost at Philippi, he "encouraged the brothers and sisters" there (16:40). All anonymous, commissioned now to live out the faith in a hostile setting, in an outpost of the Kingdom of Heaven.

The excitement of the Book of Acts is in Peter's sermon at Pentecost, and in the healing that came at the temple gate via Peter and John; we find it in the miracle of Philip's conversation on a wilderness road with an Ethiopian government official, and in the magnificent travels of Paul. But without the anonymous apostles, there is no story: no Puteoli or Ptolemais, no sustaining church after the apostles have gone on to another city.

We continue to look, in our day, for the landmark biblical scholars, the exciting evangelist, the church leader with new ideas. We ought to pay more attention to the anonymous saints. There is no church, no future, without them.

1 0

The Irreducible Message

The Christian church was born in a time and culture when the marketplace of beliefs was crowded to its borders. Religion was everywhere. Perhaps we should call it an amalgam of religion, philosophy, and superstition because it was often hard to tell one from another. At any rate, beliefs were to be found everywhere.

Paul saw as much when he entered the city of Athens. Rome was the political capital of the world, but Athens was the intellectual center. It was in Athens that new ideas were put to the test, and at that time religion was a primary issue with the thinking classes. Like us, they talked sports, politics, and economics, but religion was an everyday, everywhere issue. So what Paul saw in Athens was that "the city was flooded with idols" (Acts 17:16). He entered into the discussions immediately, not only with the people on the street but also with the philosophers on Mars Hill. Some dismissed him as "a proclaimer of foreign gods" (17:18).

They didn't find this offensive because they liked variety in their religion. Besides, so many of the thinking class in Athens were religious and philosophical dilettantes, who "used to spend their time doing nothing but talking about or listening to the newest thing" (17:21).

This meant that it was easy to talk religion, but also that it was difficult for the discussion to get serious. Religion was an idea to be played with; it provided an intellectual game, with opportunities for clever repartee and playful jousting of minds, but little more. People didn't bet their lives on such matters. They operated on the principle that each person had a right to his or her opinions and they to theirs, and to best another person in such a religious discussion didn't necessarily mean any sort of conversion, but simply that you had couched your insights more effectively or cleverly than the other person.

No wonder, then, that the followers of Christ were known as the "people of the Way." Theirs was not simply a new philosophy to be thrown into this marketplace of ideas, but a way of life. Indeed, a way of life and death. Their religion was dreadfully serious in its intentions; yet somehow its followers were marked by their joy. It was enough to bewilder any philosophical dilettante. The marvel is that it survived. As we might say today, it appealed because it was counterintuitive. It is as if the apostles had said, "What is it that is most *unlikely* to appeal to people," and finding that theme, went out to sell it.

So they often had to do it in a hurry. The apostles (of whatever shape or size) didn't have time to set up theological seminaries or Bible training institutes, nor could they leave behind a textbook summarizing their basic beliefs. Paul and others like him would stay for a week or a month, sometimes for a year or more. But mostly what people knew was from sermons and sometimes from what we today might call faith testimonies. And usually, followed up with intense house-gatherings in homes where believers gathered to pray, worship, and learn.

The classic, summarized declaration of faith came on the Day of Pentecost. The crowd that assembled was an almost entirely Jewish audience, with perhaps a few Gentiles who had chosen to accept circumcision and Judaism. They were pilgrims who had come to Jerusalem to celebrate the Pentecost festival, along with the residents of Jerusalem. They listened to the ecstatic words of the upper room group out of curiosity, but curiosity with substance: they heard these people "declaring the mighty works of God" in the languages of their homelands (2:11). So when the time came for an extended report, the apostle Peter gave them a text from what was for them an authentic source, the prophet Joel. Peter told them that now God was speaking, as Joel had predicted, by pouring out his Spirit on all flesh.

Then he moved into a brief, vigorous declaration of doctrine. For all he knew at that moment, this might be his only time to tell the story. I venture that this sense of immediacy—"Let me tell you while I have the chance!"—was the emotional and theological trademark of much preaching in the first generation of the faith. Many of the early witnesses were propelled by the conviction that Christ might return at any time, but all by the feeling that they must tell their story while they had the chance. What they had to say was uniquely important because it was crucial to life as it should be lived at that moment and crucial to their eternal welfare.

So what did Peter say? That Jesus the Nazarene, "a man whose credentials God proved to you through miracles, wonders, and signs, which God performed through him among you," they had "killed by nailing him to a cross." This, however, was according to "God's established plan and foreknowledge." But this was not the end of the story. "God raised him up! God freed him from death's dreadful grip, since it was impossible for death to hang on to him" (2:22-24). At this point, Peter substantiated his word by quoting David (Psalm 16:8-11) and insisting that "David spoke about the resurrection of Christ" (Acts 2:31).

Now Peter became even more daring. This Jesus has been "exalted to God's right side and received from the Father the promised Holy Spirit," the evidence of which they had now seen. "Beyond question...God has made this Jesus, whom you crucified, both Lord and Christ" (2:33, 36). When the crowd asked Peter what they should do, he instructed them to change their hearts and lives and "be baptized in the name of Jesus Christ for the forgiveness of your sins" (2:38). About three thousand did so that day.

Peter had given them a short course in the theology of the Way. He did so by way of the Hebrew Scriptures, the Old Testament. As for what we now call the New Testament, it was coming to birth before the eyes and ears of the crowd, without their knowing it, with its roots solidly set in the Old. He told the crowd that though they had crucified Jesus, this crucifixion was in God's plan. Now God had raised Jesus from the dead (again, as anticipated in the Hebrew Scriptures), and Jesus was now positioned on equality with God, and had sent the Holy Spirit into the world (again, according to the Hebrew Scriptures).

There would be refinements and expositions on the message in time soon to follow, but here surely were some irreducibles. The believers were not without a book; they were the inheritors of the Hebrew Scriptures. One key item would be removed; circumcision would not be required for the people of God, as it had been for the nation of Israel. Many dietary and cultural practices would be explicitly denied later by remarkable experiences that would be recorded in the Book of Acts, and others that would be superseded by teachings in the Gospels. Often the apostolic letters reinforced Old Testament laws regarding moral conduct. The Jews had a strict moral code very unlike the indifferent morality of the first-century world, and neither the Book of Acts nor the letters abandoned those standards.

Then, in a sweeping summary Peter identified the person of Jesus the Nazarene: his crucifixion, his resurrection, and his full identity with God. And with this he went on to declare that God's Holy Spirit had come into the world for the benefit of all of God's people. Peter announced that a new time had come; God was doing a new thing that had begun with sending his Son into the world, then raising him from the dead, and now sending the Holy Spirit. Peter gave a succinct, powerful statement, based on the teachings as he now understood them from the Psalms and the prophets.

Acts gives us another such summary by way of Paul's early preaching and teaching in his ministry at Antioch in Pisidia. Paul's sermon at the synagogue there was preceded by a reading from the Law and the Prophets, as would be customary in a synagogue service. When Paul had opportunity to speak he began like Peter at Pentecost and Stephen before the Jerusalem Council, with a history of God's work with the Jews. And as at Pentecost, Paul proceeded from there to Jesus' crucifixion and resurrection. Like Peter, he supported his case with quotations from the Hebrew Scriptures (13:38-39).

We instinctively expect these early sermons to include some quotations from Jesus' teachings—perhaps from the Sermon on the Mount, or certain key parables or teachings on the Kingdom of God. Or explicit reference to the healings Jesus performed or to his miracles. Instead, however, these early sermons by the apostles concentrated on the crucifixion and resurrection of our Lord, and in the nature of his identity with God. In this respect the sermons in Acts are like the Apostles' Creed, which moves from Jesus' conception and birth to his trial before Pilate and his crucifixion and resurrection, with no mention of his ministry, his miracles, or his teachings.

One might expect that these sermons would ease people into theology, so to speak. The crucifixion raised questions about Jesus as a citizen (that is, why would the Roman government crucify him). As for the resurrection, naturally this was difficult for critical thinkers to accept. Nevertheless, when Paul entered into the dialogue of ideas with the philosophers and theologians of Athens, he began with what was the most basic and also the most difficult to accept. He praised the people of Athens for being "very religious in every way," even to the point of having an image to "an unknown God" (17:22-23). Then, with a grand sweep he described God as having a stake in all of the human race, so that in God "we live, move, and exist," quoting one of their own poets in support of what he was saying (17:28). At that point, however, he dared to attack the graven images that populated the city streets, because now God was going to "judge the world justly by a man he has appointed. God has given proof of this to everyone by raising him from the dead" (17:31). Paul took the most controversial element in the Jesus story in speaking to the most critical audience. Logic says that he would hold this issue for a later time, after some areas of agreement had been established. Not so, because the resurrection was at the heart of all he had to say.

Paul was passionate about what he included in his teaching. There was nothing incidental about it. When he bade farewell to the leaders at Ephesus he declared that he was "not responsible for anyone's fate. I haven't avoided proclaiming the entire plan of God to you" (20:26-27). He reminded them that he was leaving them "to shepherd God's church, which he obtained with the death of his own

Son" (20:28). Here, again, the crucifixion and its saving power. Paul then warned that "savage wolves" (20:29) would come among them, with false teachings. Paul and the other apostles would have been astonished at an attitude of laissez faire, which we now rather often take for granted in religious discussions, where believers accept what they find comfortable and lay the rest aside.

Obviously we don't know everything Paul had in mind when he reminded the Ephesians that he had proclaimed "the entire plan of God" to them. But from the Book of Acts, we know that he, like Peter, found several matters altogether basic: that Christ had been crucified to a purpose and not simply as a victim of trumped-up charges and a faltering Pilate, and that this crucifixion was made ridiculous by Jesus' resurrection. He, like Peter, found the basis for his understanding in the Hebrew Scriptures; it wasn't something recently trumped up by a band of pathetic heretics.

And all of this was to show itself in a way of life. No wonder that the believers were first called the people of the Way! They were not enunciating a philosophy to like or dislike, to believe or disbelieve, but a way to live, really live. So truly so, in fact, that not to live this way was to die, to miss life altogether.

The apostolic letters—especially Paul's—would add a variety of details about any number of subjects. Indeed, the range is as wide as the issues of daily living, because they resulted from the problems, the questions, and the failures of the early believers. Galatians dealt almost exclusively with the issue of faith and works: that is, how much does our salvation depend on our works and on God's grace (how amazing, really, is grace?)—specifically, whether the work of the cross was sufficient for salvation or whether one must also come under the Law of Moses. The letters to the Corinthians covered issues as diverse as conduct in public worship and taking fellow believers to court. Thessalonians dealt with numbers of questions having to do with Christ's return. And woven through it all were Paul's very personal, very transparent expressions of his love for his people and his concern for their spiritual welfare. The Letters of John and Jude confront the heresies that were seeking the support of early believers. Most if not all of these epistles were written before the Book of Acts, but Acts records the story of the birth and establishing of "the people of the Way," those extraordinary days when the church was young.

To the best of our knowledge the epistles also preceded the writing of the four Gospels, and of course Luke's Gospel was written before the Acts. It is in the Gospels that we get the record of our Lord's birth, his teachings, and his ministry, with a disproportionate amount of time given to the final days of his life: Jesus' trial, crucifixion, and resurrection. When we see how much space is given to the end of Jesus' life and to the resurrection, we realize that Peter and Paul and the first preachers/teachers were consistent in their emphasis on these subjects.

But why? Why didn't the early sermons say more about the Kingdom of God, which was so paramount in John the

Baptist's message and his way-preparing for Jesus, and so much a part of Jesus' teaching? Why so much about the crucifixion? Paul readily confesses, in his First Letter to Corinth, that the message of the cross was not appealing. It wasn't an "easy sell," to put the issue in the language of our public relations, product-appealing world. Paul divided the world into two parts, Jews and Gentiles, and admitted that the cross didn't appeal to either one: it was a "scandal to Jews and foolishness to Gentiles" (1 Corinthians 1:23). No matter; for Paul the cross was the passionate center of his preaching, because "to those who are called—both Jews and Greeks—Christ is God's power and God's wisdom." And this "foolishness of God is wiser than human wisdom, and the weakness of God is stronger than human strength" (1:24-25).

As for the resurrection, the apostles saw this as God's vindication of the plan of salvation. Jesus had walked unafraid into the place and face of death. More than that, he had taken upon himself the *cause* of death, which is sin. It would have been meaningless for anyone else to volunteer to take the burden of sin for others since each of us has sins of his own to bear. But as the apostolic writer put it later, Jesus "was tempted in every way that we are, except without sin" (Hebrews 4:15). Thus he came now, "at the end of the ages to get rid of sin by sacrificing himself" (9:26), and in doing so took upon himself the death of all humanity.

If he had remained dead, however, death (and with it, sin) would have become the ultimate conqueror. Not so, for on the third day of his abode in the place of the dead, he was resurrected. The crucifixion and the resurrection were both essential parts of the Christ story. Whatever else might be said of him—teacher, example, or even person of extraordinary birth—nothing was so essential to his story as this, that he was crucified, went to the place of death, and on the third day rose again.

There was much more to be said, much of it drawn from the Hebrew Scriptures that the early believers saw fulfilled in him, much in his unexcelled teachings, and much in the clarifying and exalting language of the epistles. But here was the irreducible, whether at the Day of Pentecost when the church was born, or as Paul would declare it in his preaching to a mixed crowd at Antioch or to the querulous skeptics at Mars Hill. Other things were important, vitally so because they undergirded the basics; but whatever else, this unlikely combination, this hard-to-swallow message: he was crucified according to the Scriptures and on the third day was raised by the power of God. Beginning there, the first declarers of the story set out to conquer the world.

1 1

The Shaping of Doctrine

One reason Jesus appeals to many people is their feeling that he kept religion simple. "Love God, and love your neighbor": Jesus said that therein lay all the teachings of the law and the prophets. We like to have life and its issues condensed into half-a-dozen words. Whether we're struggling with the Internal Revenue Code on April 15, trying to explain to a teenager why it's important to do what is right, or wrestling through some issue in our own souls in the hours just before dawn, we'd like if possible to get the whole story in capsule form. Jesus seemed to offer that, not only in his teachings (as we sometimes perceive them) but also in his person. Here is grace for our sins, here is our new way of life, here is our hope in time and eternity. No wonder Jesus appeals to us.

For the same reason, the apostle Paul is unappealing to many. Some fret that Paul changed Jesus' simple, loving teachings into complicated theological issues that are difficult to understand and that sometimes seem obtuse and not worthy of discussion. At the same time, however, what sometimes bothers us about Paul are those teachings that are easy to understand (or that seem so) and that offend us.

We'd like to keep it simple. It became popular in the late twentieth century, whether the subject was politics, economics, or family life, to summarize any problem by reminding ourselves, "The devil is in the details." But that's not quite fair. Here's the fact of the matter: life is lived out in details. Love is beautiful, but we experience it in daily relationships that are numerous, sometimes hurried, and often tedious. That is, details. Eternity is what we're made for, but our introduction to eternity on this earth is in momentary pieces.

And of course Jesus didn't stop with the simple rule, "love God, love neighbor." He reminded us that the laws for loving neighbor go deeper than murder and adultery. Lust after someone in our hearts, and we've entered the realm of adultery; call another person a fool, and we're welcoming murder into our hearts and thoughts and vocabulary. Jesus spoke of self-righteousness and humility, of responsibility to the poor and of the dangers of riches, and of how fearfully difficult it is to enter the kingdom of heaven. And these aren't simple.

No wonder, then, that doctrine began to take shape as soon as Peter delivered the first Christian sermon on the Day of Pentecost. And no wonder that it began, as we've already noted, with texts from the Hebrew Scriptures. The church may have been born on Pentecost, but its birthday was on a Hebrew holy day. The roots of Christianity were in the promises made to Abraham, Isaac, and Jacob; promises that were then developed and clarified in the history of Israel and in the teachings of the psalms and the prophets.

Pause here long enough to underline this statement: If the twenty-first-century church is to regain the wonder of the first century, it must regain its Old Testament roots. The four Gospels are not enough, nor are the epistles, and certainly not the Revelation. The church is a continuation of Israel and its grand calling from God. We can never be a New Testament church without our Old Testament roots. We will never be the new people of God without acknowledging with humility our dependence on Abraham, Isaac, Jacob, Moses, David, Isaiah, and Amos, to name a few.

But we need also to know that we do not stop there. Our roots are there, yes, but we are now the plant and the place of fruit. So Jesus demanded a higher way: "Don't even begin to think that I have come to do away with the Law and the Prophets. I haven't come to do away with them but to fulfill them.... You have heard that it was said to those who lived long ago, *Don't commit murder* ...But I say to you that everyone who is angry with their brother or sister will be in danger of judgment" (Matthew 5:17, 21, 22).

So it was, then, that the early apostolic sermons began with the Old Testament and made Jesus the issue. In Corinth, for instance, Paul and his team began their mission in the synagogue, as was their custom. And what did he say? "Paul devoted himself fully to the word, testifying to the Jews that Jesus was the Christ" (Acts 18:5). When they rejected this message, Paul declared, "From now on I'll go to the Gentiles" (18:6). Because Jesus was the way of salvation, he was the issue. A sharp line was being drawn. It had to have been a painfully divisive line for Paul, passionate Jew that he was, but Paul knew not only the roots of his faith in Judaism but also the faith that must now grow from those roots.

Christianity's roots in Judaism became an issue for the early believers. An ethnic factor was also at work here. Judaism belonged to the Jews, yet soon those coming into the church were increasingly from the Gentile world. This added an intangible but real element to the conflict. The apostles needed to know what parts of Judaism carried over into life in the Way and what did not. We've already seen how earnestly and prayerfully the leaders in Jerusalem struggled with these matters and with what grace they settled early discussions.

As we've also noted, however, Jerusalem edicts didn't fully settle matters. Paul's letter to the people in Galatia makes clear that those who saw Christ as somehow only a partial savior—that is, with salvation supplemented by the laws of Moses, particularly circumcision—sought to win Paul's converts to their practices. The principle that was involved—law versus grace—is so fundamental that it was the primary issue fifteen centuries later in Martin Luther's revolt against Roman Catholicism. Which is to say, doctrine is not just a study of historical thought, it is a continuing fact in the living out of the Christian faith century after century. When it comes to heresy, there's little new under the sun.

The Letters of John show this at another point of issue, the nature of Christ. As the creeds would state it, Jesus was very God of very God and very man of very man; he was both human and divine. Today the issue is likely to be the divinity of Jesus, but in the first century the heresy was that Jesus was not really human but only seemed to be: "Many deceivers have gone into the world who do not confess that Jesus Christ came as a human being. This kind of person is the deceiver and the antichrist" (2 John 7). To such John declared, "We announce to you what existed from the beginning, what we have heard, what we have seen with our eyes, what we have seen and our hands handled, about the word of life" (1 John 1:1).

The epistles came into existence to cope with the questions that were common in the early church. They were doctrinal questions. Some were at the most pedestrian level of ordinary daily living, and some of a quality that would have delighted the savants at Mars Hill. And as surely as some came out of the transition from Judaism to Christianity, many more came by way of introducing the Way of Christ to the pagan culture of the Gentile world. Theirs was a world of many beliefs, most of which were dispensable for convenience sake. For the people of the Way, however, who knew Jesus Christ as the Way, the Truth, and the Life, beliefs were eternally significant in this world and the next. Beliefs were not judged by the standard of "some new thought" but of the morality, the integrity, and the ultimate beauty of life in Christ. This Christ who had redeemed them was not one among many, but the only Way, and to choose him meant also the possibility of dying for him, as persecutions became more frequent and more violent.

Ironically, the church owes much to the heretics who compelled the apostles to draw lines of clear, sharp, and sometimes painful distinction. Who is this Jesus the Christ? Paul answered that "he was in the form of God...being equal with God" (Philippians 2:6); "the image of the invisible God, the one who is first over all creation...all things were created through him and for him. He existed before all things, and all things are held together in him" (Colossians 1:15-17). And what does this mean to us? "We have been ransomed through his...blood, and we have forgiveness for our failures based on his overflowing grace" (Ephesians 1:7).

And how ought we then to live? "So put to death the parts of your life that belong to the earth, such as sexual immorality, moral corruption, lust, evil desire, and greed (which is idolatry)....But now set aside these things, such as anger, rage, malice, slander, and obscene language" (Colossians 3:5, 8). And what ought our final aim to be? "God's goal is for us to become mature adults—to be fully grown, measured by the standard of the fullness of Christ" (Ephesians 4:13).

Paul didn't have two theologies, one for philosophical discussion and the other for daily living. It was all of one piece. Thus he moved with hardly a pause from the grandeur of the Christ who is "equal with God" to an appeal for Euodia and Syntyche "to come to an agreement in the Lord," and to ask their fellow believers to "help these women" who had been his coworkers in the gospel (Philippians 2:6; 4:2-3). And because we belong to one who "existed before all things" we should have nothing to do with sexual immorality, moral corruption, anger, rage, malice, slander, and obscene language (Colossians 1:17; 3:5, 8).

Does it seem anticlimactic, almost amusing, to hear Paul follow up talk about the majesty of Christ by urging believers, so to speak, to "watch their tongues"? Not to Paul. This Gospel is all of òne piece. It is a grand, eternal salvation, and it is lived out in the market place of chatter. Christ is God's Savior, and we obey him even in the bed of sexual activity. And he is the Savior of all humankind, thus there is no difference between Jew and Gentile, male and female, slave and free. Or to put it in our twenty-first-century venues, there is no difference between the part-time worker at the fast food window and the mul-timillionaire who lunches in the private executive club, no difference between the scholar who feels at home in polysyllabic discussion and the man who testifies, "Jesus loves me, this I know, for the Bible tells me so." As the saying goes, the land is level at the Cross. This is a gospel that reaches us where we are, and that calls upon us to live it out where we live.

That is: the first-century believers were already widely referred to as "the people of the Way"; now Paul and the other first-century preachers were spelling out the nature of the Way, the particulars by which those observing the believers would know that our Way is, in fact, the Way that bears the Savior's name. And a Way that demands lives that are consistent with their doctrine.

It was the business of the apostles, named and unnamed, to spell out this faith as they preached to commoners and kings, shopkeepers and slaves, women and men and youth. Then, after they had left a community in the charge of some of those believers in towns known today only by archaeologists, with some yet to be discovered, the apostles would receive questions: some profound, some almost amusingly pragmatic.

Most of the answers have come to us through the letters of Paul. In a sense, this is logical. He was a trained scholar, a rabbi in his own right, a man who was at home in Athens, though he was put off by their multiple gods and perhaps by their tendency to structure everything in obtuse language. On the other hand, however, his very gifted mind could have gotten in the way. How can a scholar of such proportions speak to the commonality of the human race?

This is where Paul, the ultimate pastor, shines. He possessed a heart for people that impelled him in all that he did. Did he learn this as he worked the marketplace as a tentmaker and leather worker? Or is it something he got in his several years with Barnabas, that master encourager?

However it happened, I'm impressed that Luke tells us that when Paul and Silas left the prison in Philippi, they "made their way to Lydia's house where they *encouraged* the brothers and sisters" (Acts 16:40; italics mine). After trying days in Ephesus when Paul might have been glad simply to shake the dust from his sandals, instead "Paul sent for the disciples, *encouraged* them, said good-bye, and left for the province of Macedonia" (20:1, italics mine). He proceeded then to travel "through that region with a message of *encouragement*" (20:2, italics mine).

Mind you, a pastor must sometimes admonish, correct, instruct, and even rebuke; but above all, the pastor must encourage. Like the prophet before him, the pastor must be able to say, "I sat where they sat." One can't experience every person's pain and pleasure, sorrow and laughter, but he or she must have a gift of capacity and a willingness to make every person's experience his own. Especially, a pastor must have a heart for the other person's journey.

I doubt that this came easily to Paul. By nature and heritage, he was an achiever. He didn't study under Gamaliel to be mediocre, nor did he seek early to be a Pharisee because he loved the comfortable, middle ground. He aimed always for life's Everest. But he found himself preaching to broken human beings, to average folk (if there are such) who struggled with average problems. Of course no problem is average when it is one's own problem; no incline is an easy slope when it comes at a peculiar time in the journey. And never more so than for those to whom Paul preached, people who were converts to a Way of life that called for more than their best and that often made them outcasts not only within their surrounding culture but even within their own families. As Paul came to such people, he *encouraged* them, and when he left them it was with the same gracious word.

Doctrine coldly delivered is far removed from encouragement. Doctrine is demanding to both mind and spirit. It raises a high bar that sometimes also becomes a separating barrier. Those who preach and teach doctrine had better be encouragers or their teaching will break the spirit—or worse, harden it—while challenging the mind. If Barnabas was the Son of Encouragement, Paul surely became the Grandson of Encouragement. It was from that platform that he spelled out his theology. Whether in the lofty insights of Christology or the straightforward statements of daily conduct, Paul delivered his doctrine with a pastor's heart. Though a scholar by nature, he was a craftsman by daily occupation. He learned, masterfully, to combine the two.

But doctrine was never unimportant and certainly never dispensable. To follow one who said, "I am the Truth" left no room for careless thinking. And for those who fear that truth seems sometimes to be unloving, two words should be spoken. First, that there is no love in falsehood, because falsehood is a deceiver. To love is therefore to speak the truth. But just as surely, truth dare never be taught without love. To speak truth hatefully or arrogantly or with intention to put down another is to deny its very essence. When truth is spoken without love, it loses its essential quality.

It was a difficult assignment; only saints could manage it and in their humanness Christians sometimes fell short. Without truth—that is, without doctrine—the church would very shortly lose its way. Nevertheless, doctrine itself is a barrier to those who choose not to decide or who feel they are in the process of finding their way.

Statistically, that group is growing in America. Respected surveys show that between 1990 and 2010 the number of those who claimed no religious affiliation increased from 14 million to 46 million. They are not only the fastest growing "religions" group in the United States, but they now also outnumber those belonging to mainline Protestant bodies in America. Many are very serious about their religious thinking, but no longer identify. It is not unfair to think of them as that part of the first-century world that made an altar to "an unknown god."

Meanwhile, in Acts and the epistles the people of the Way drew up the body of doctrine that became the bedrock foundation of Christian belief. To believe in the Way, the Truth, and the Life required a structure of certainty.

1 2

The Maps of Paul and Several Others

If your Bible includes a section of maps there will almost surely be one or more tracing the travels of the apostle Paul. He discovered no new countries, planted no flags on conquered territories, and led no exploratory expeditions, yet his travels may well have resulted in more travel maps for the average person than any king or explorer. And this in spite of the fact that his travels covered only a relatively small area, sections surrounding and inland from the Mediterranean Sea.

It's strange that he left behind such a geographer's record. Much credit goes to Luke, the author of Acts. Evidently Luke himself was part of Paul's team on numbers of these trips, as indicated by his slipping into the first person plural on several occasions, beginning in Acts 16:10: "Immediately after he [Paul] saw the vision, _we_ prepared to leave for the province of

Macedonia, concluding that God had called u̲s̲ to proclaim the good news to them" (italics mine). And as Luke is bringing his book to a close at a setting in Rome where Paul "lived in his own rented quarters for two full years" (Acts 28:30) he introduces the section in the same first person plural language: "When *we* entered Rome, Paul was permitted to live by himself, with a soldier guarding him" (28:16).

So yes, the biblical historian was living many of Paul's travels with him; thus the full and intimate record. But there's the prior question: how is it that Paul became Christianity's most notable traveler, the one who led the way in breaking ethnic, social, and religious barriers, and the first to follow a call into Macedonia, to what would become the western world of Christendom?

There's a divine answer, and we ought to notice it first because it introduces us to the purposes of God in Paul's life and to Paul's unique place in the church. When God instructed Ananias to visit Saul immediately after Saul's encounter with Christ on the road to Damascus, the assignment began with urgency: "Go!" Then, the reason for the urgency: "This man is the agent I have chosen to carry my name before Gentiles, kings, and Israelites" (9:15).

Only God knows the purposes of God, and when we humans speculate upon those purposes, we're not only traveling in matters beyond our depth, we're gambling on reasoning where human reasons don't necessarily apply. True, Paul knew the Gentile world beyond the experience of the original followers of Jesus. At the same time, however, he was a Pharisee, the body of Jews with the most passionate loyalty to everything in their Jewish tradition. One might say that Paul knew the Gentiles well enough to know how superior it was to be a Jew. But Paul's conversion was not only a powerful turning-around from persecutor to advocate, it was equally miraculous that this most loyal and proudest of Jews should be the one chosen to serve as the apostle to the Gentiles. No wonder, then, that Luke brings his story to a close by still another report of something that happened quite often in Paul's ministry.

As Acts reports it, Paul began his work in Rome by seeking out the Jewish community, so he could explain that it was "because of the hope of Israel that I am bound with this chain." They responded that they knew nothing of what he was doing except that "people everywhere are speaking against this faction." With that, from "morning until evening" Paul "explained and testified concerning God's kingdom and tried to convince them about Jesus through appealing to the Law of Moses and the Prophets." Some were convinced but others "refused to believe." As the group prepared to leave, Paul warned them in the words of the prophet Isaiah that they were doing just what their ancestors had done, in rejecting the witness of God. Since they were rejecting God's salvation, this salvation "has been sent to the Gentiles. They will listen!" (Acts 28:20, 22-24, 28). Thus Acts concludes by Paul's declaring the depth of his conviction about his ministry to the Gentiles. Paul writes to the Romans, "Brothers and sisters, my heart's desire is for Israel's salvation" (Romans 10:1), so much so that he would be willing to be "cursed, cut off from Christ" if it could mean their salvation (Romans 9:3). Nevertheless, his calling was beyond the Jews.

So he traveled!

> I was shipwrecked three times. I spent a day and a night on the open sea. I've been on many jour-neys. I faced dangers from rivers, robbers, my people, and Gentiles. I faced dangers in the city, in the desert, on the sea, and from false brothers and sisters. I faced these dangers with hard work and heavy labor, many sleepless nights, hunger and thirst, often without food, and in the cold without enough clothes. (2 Corinthians 11:25-27)

Paul didn't travel first class. There were no luxury hotels. He was a man on a mission.

Ironically, he was also one who—unwittingly—sent out missioners before he was himself converted. It seems clear in the opening chapters of Acts that while the temple authorities were disturbed and were doing all they could to control the situation, they were avoiding violent action against the new sect. But Stephen's sermon and his ston-ing death by the council members changed everything. "At that time, the church in Jerusalem began to be subjected to vicious harassment. Everyone except the apostles was scat-tered throughout the regions of Judea and Samaria" (Acts 8:1). At this point Saul (later to be Paul) rose to leadership in the persecution. He "began to wreak havoc against the church. Entering one house after another, he would drag off both men and women and throw them into prison"

(8:3). And what happened when he did so? "Those who had been scattered moved on, preaching the good news along the way" (8:4). Paul was an unintentional missionary executive, sending out preachers helter-skelter, all the while he was trying to silence the message.

I bring us back to this part of the story because it was so clearly a turning point in the life and witness of the church. Jesus had commissioned his disciples to begin in Jerusalem but then to go into the adjoining areas of Judea and Samaria and from there into all the world. Beginning at Pentecost, however, there was something idyllic about Jerusalem. Souls were being saved daily, miracles were commonplace, and love and generosity were the order of the day. It's as if the believers calculated that the world would come to them. It had been so on Pentecost; why shouldn't Jerusalem be the capital of the Kingdom, where unbelievers could come and be changed? Instead of going into all the world, the world could come to them.

But Stephen's speech changed all of that, followed by Saul's passion for wiping out the movement. And with it, "everyone except the apostles was scattered" (8:1). First it was Judea and Samaria, but then it was Antioch— and then, clearly, wherever the believers went, they were "preaching the good news along the way" (8:4). The missionary movement had begun, propelled by persecution. Persecution could drive the believers out of Jerusalem, but it couldn't drive the commitment and passion out of the believers. Instead of silencing the movement, persecution empowered it.

Short of heaven, we will never know where these people went or who they were. Traditions and legends have come to us about the apostles, as we noted earlier, but what kind of legends do we have about believers who fled to given villages and set up outposts of the kingdom? The villages themselves are lost to history, without enough potsherds to offer an archaeological story; if the villages themselves are lost, what shall we say for the persons who carried the gospel to them?

Philip Jenkins, one of the preeminent historians of our time, writes of the lost history of Christianity. He reminds us that as late as the eleventh century, "Asia was still home to at least a third of the world's Christians," and that Mesopotamia (Iraq) "retained a powerful Christian culture at least through the thirteenth century. In terms of the number and splendor of its churches and monasteries, its vast scholarship and dazzling spirituality, Iraq was through the late Middle Ages at least as much a cultural and spiritual heartland of Christianity as was France or Germany, or indeed Ireland."[1] We think today of certain Asian and north African countries as exclusively Muslim, not realizing that they were once strongholds of Christianity. If we have all but lost record of the church of less than a millennium ago, how can we imagine the villages, the cities, the territories where our spiritual ancestors went with the faith in the generation of Paul and the apostles, and in the century just following? And who can say what towering souls led the way in that first century—great, simple, convinced folk who did their work in farm or marketplace, as slave or artisan, then gathered in the evening and on Sabbaths to sing their faith?

In those days to win a soul was more likely than not to also win a household, including not only physical family but also workers, servants, or slaves. One sees that principle in action in the story of the jailer at Philippi: "He and everyone in his household were immediately baptized" (Acts 16:33). It's interesting to see how often reference is made not simply to a believer but also to that person's "household." This reflects the cohesive nature of family and vocational life in that world, but also the holy contagion of conversion. After noting that the jailer's household was baptized, Acts goes on to report that the jailer was "overjoyed because he and everyone in his household had come to believe in God" (16:34).

No wonder the church grew. And no wonder that when persecutions came, whether in the days of Saul's preconversion or in the many that followed intermittently, so many believers who were driven from their homes simply became interim missionaries or evangelists in their new homes. Perhaps many started a company of believers in their home where in time a person within the new faith community was slowly recognized as having the gift of a pastor, and by authority of the Holy Spirit became the continuing leader of the group. This growth was a wondrous thing. It was nothing less, as Peter recognized at Pentecost, than God's outpouring of the Holy Spirit on "all people...your sons and daughters...your young...your elders...my servants" (2:17-18).

Who can map these people? Who can say where they went, what churches they started, how many of those house churches survived into larger congregations, and how many failed to take hold? With the help of the Book of Acts we can follow Paul through his untiring venture into at least some of his territories and cities, but how could we begin to draw up a map or a series of maps that would show the spread of the Gospel in its earliest generations?

It is one thing, however, to win a city, a village, a neighborhood, or a family, and quite another to keep it. Somehow it's more difficult to keep the fires of faith alive in a second or third generation than to make a new convert in an otherwise pagan world. America's Puritan ancestors discovered as much. They tried with a holy resolve to make sure their children believed. Part of the Sabbath celebration in the early American Puritan household, as J. I. Packer has explained, was for the head of the house to catechize the children during the afternoon to see if they had grasped the morning sermon.[2] This effort was earnest, sincere, and no doubt well done. Nevertheless, there came a time when parents conceded a measure of defeat, with the installation of the Halfway Covenant. This ruling held that if a person couldn't testify to a conversion experience yet held to the teachings of the church, they could have partial membership but without the right to receive communion or to vote.

One wonders if the first-century church ever had such a "partial" arrangement. When parents have come into faith by a memorable experience, via their own "Damascus

Road," they want nothing less for their children. But it isn't easy to transfer faith from one generation to another, as the history of religious awakenings and renewals demonstrate repeatedly. Nevertheless, current studies in American religious life testify dramatically to the power of this influence in our own time. "Mothers and fathers who practice what they preach and preach what they practice are far and away the biggest influence related to adolescents keeping the faith into their twenties, according to new findings from a landmark study of youth and religion." Of children raised by parents who talk their faith at home, attach importance to their beliefs, and are active in their congregations, 82 percent are religiously active as young adults, whereas this is true of only 1 percent of fifteen- to seventeen-year-olds from homes where the parents attach little importance to religion.[3]

All of which is to say that the map of faith is not easy to trace, or to maintain. There's no "divine right of faith" to compare with the historic divine right of kings; one doesn't become a Christian automatically because one's parents were. Nor is a congregation born in the fires of religious fervor or of the enthusiasm of a dynamic leader assured that twenty years later the same holy vigor will still be present. The Spirit of God is not subject to committee action or to even the best intentions of yesterday's leaders. The memory can still be there, and a wistfulness for the "good old days," but these do not take the place of a faith owned by contemporaries committed to serving their own time.

For those of us living in the western world, our greatest challenge is twofold. First, to find the reality of the Book of Acts for the time in which we live, and second, to pass it on to a new generation with an integrity they cannot resist.

But can we expect that the Acts story is still relevant nearly two millennia later? Or is it unrepeatable, with stories we can cherish and envy but not expect to replicate?

I believe the Acts story has been repeated, in its original reality and power, at a variety of times and places. Sometimes the place has been small (a village or perhaps only a congregation of believers); sometimes a nation (as in the Wesleyan revival of the eighteenth century), and sometimes within a kind of sociological community larger than a geographical one (as in the Businessmen's Revival of 1857–1858). From what I read and hear, it is happening in our time in great sections of Africa, South America, and Asia.

But can it happen in the United States or Canada or western Europe? Can it break through our spiritual ennui, our preoccupation with material and scientific progress, and our laissez-faire attitude toward the eternal?

Yes, I'm sure it can. Sure, because I believe the basic needs of humanity are the same; only the cultures have changed. I believe, too, in the calling of the church. If we are, as Paul's generation believed, the body of Christ in the world, and if Christ is the reality we believe him to be, then the church—however faltering it is and always has been—will rise to the occasion. Still faltering at times, still disappointing us, still reminding us by its conduct that it is made up of persons like ourselves, but nevertheless the Body of Christ.

I believe that the story in Acts is a continuing story. Luke, who was a reliable historian and a sensitive storyteller, didn't write a conclusion to Acts. Paul was still receiving followers, inquirers, and skeptics as the story stops. Just as, at our best, we are still doing today. Paul's maps were finished, but the other mapmakers in the Book of Acts were still at work as Acts ended. And now our mapmakers, as represented by the best of us in the twenty-first century, are still going strong, still translating the story into new dialects and languages, still seeing miracles small and larger (recognized and more often not), and still living out the faith as our Lord told us to do: in Jerusalem, Samaria and Judea, and to the uttermost parts of the world. And the uttermost boundaries of human time as we know it, too. We are still making new maps and will continue to do so.

Amen, and Amen.

Notes

1. Some Extraordinary, Unremarkable People

1. J. B. Phillips, *The Young Church in Action* (London: Collins, 1955, 1959), 11–12.

3. People of the Great Heart

1. G. K. Chesterton, *St. Francis of Assisi* (London: Hodder & Stoughton, 1923), 54.

4. And of Course There Were Hypocrites

1. William Lecky, *History of European Morals from Augustus to Charlemagne* (London: Longmans, 1869), 394.

5. Did the Apostles Make a Mistake?

1. John Fox, *Book of Martyrs; or, a History of the Lives, Sufferings, and Triumphant Deaths of the Primitive as Well as Protestant Martyrs: from the Commencement of Christianity to the Latest Periods of Pagan and Popish Persecution* (Hartford, CT: Edwin Hunt, 1845), 27.

2. Roland Bainton, *Here I Stand* (Nashville: Abingdon, 1950), 154.

7. The Slow Process of Tumbling Walls

1. William Barclay, *The Daily Study Bible: The Acts of the Apostles* (Philadelphia: Westminster, 1953), 125.

8. The Man Who Saved the New Testament

1. William Barclay, *The Letters to Timothy, Titus, and Philemon* (Louisville: Westminster John Knox, 2003), 244.

9. The Anonymous Apostles

1. Craig S. Keener, *The IVP Bible Background Commentary New Testament (Second Edition)* (Downers Grove, IL: IVP Academic, 2014), 547.

12. The Maps of Paul and Several Others

1. Philip Jenkins, *The Lost History of Christianity* (New York: HarperOne, 2008), 4, 6.

2. J. I. Packer, *A Quest for Godliness* (Wheaton: Crossway, 1990), 241.

3. David Briggs, "Parents Are Top Influence in Teens Remaining Active in Religion as Young Adults," *Christian Century* (December 24, 2014): 17.

Study Guide
for J. Ellsworth Kalas's
The Story Continues

By John Schroeder

1. SOME EXTRAORDINARY, UNREMARKABLE PEOPLE

Summary

This chapter looks at the early believers, as seen by the apostle Paul, the odds against them, and how they carried out the work of Jesus.

Questions

1. Share your interest in this book and what you hope to gain from reading and discussing it.

2. How did the apostle Paul describe these unremarkable people?

3. Compare and contrast the Christian world then and now.

4. Why were the odds against this little body of people?

5. What does the Book of Acts tell us about this group?

6. Why is the Book of Acts so important?

7. In what ways did this group carry on the work of Jesus?

8. Why was the work of Dr. Phillips important? What insights did he offer?

9. What empowered the apostles and their followers to act?

10. What additional thoughts or ideas from this chapter would you like to explore?

Prayer

Dear God, thank you for the early believers who carried on the work of Jesus. Help us be like them and learn from them. Open our eyes and ears to the needs of others. Amen.

2. THEN THERE WAS PENTECOST

Summary

This chapter explores the story of Pentecost and how it empowered this small band of believers. It tells about the miracles that occurred and how the Holy Spirit changed everything.

Questions

1. Discuss how the resurrection of Jesus affected this small group.

2. Why was the arrival of the Holy Spirit so important to these believers?

3. Describe the miracle that happened on the Day of Pentecost.

4. Share what impresses you most from what happened that day.

5. Discuss what Peter told the gathering crowd. How were lives changed?

6. How was this band of believers empowered after Pentecost? What did members do?

7. Imagine that you were in the Upper Room that day. Share what you felt and heard.

8. What do we learn about the Holy Spirit from this event?

9. Discuss what proves the Holy Spirit is in us.

10. What additional thoughts or ideas from this chapter would you like to explore?

Prayer

Dear God, thank you for giving us Pentecost and your Holy Spirit to enrich us and the lives of others. Help us boldly share your word and love with those who need Jesus. Remind us that you are always with us as we journey through life. Amen.

3. PEOPLE OF THE GREAT HEART

Summary

This chapter tells us how and why the believers shared their possessions. It looks at the life of Barnabus, spiritual gifts, and how we should view our wealth.

Questions

1. What do we learn about individual and group potential from these followers?

2. Discuss the impact of sharing possessions in Acts 2:44 and 2:45.

3. How does having faith change your view of possessions?

4. Share a time when your eyes were opened to the needs of others.

5. How do miracles fit into our time and place?

6. Give some examples of spiritual gifts at work.

7. What impresses you about the life of Barnabas?

8. How should Christians view wealth and the power of money?

9. Share what you learned about generosity and cheerful giving from this lesson.

10. What additional thoughts or ideas from this chapter would you like to explore?

Prayer

Dear God, thank you for reminding us that our possessions are gifts from you. Help us give of ourselves, our talents, and our belongings. Open our eyes to the needy and unfortunate. May we share what we have and may we share your love. Amen.

4. AND OF COURSE THERE WERE HYPOCRITES

Summary

This chapter provides a warning about hypocrisy as illustrated in the story of Ananias and Sapphira. It illustrates the deadliness of this condition, how it hurts others, and how it damages religion.

Questions

1. How would you define *hypocrisy*? Give an example.

2. What do we learn from the story of Ananias and Sapphira?

3. Why is hypocrisy so deadly?

4. List some differences between Ananias, Sapphira, and Barnabas.

5. How and why does hypocrisy damage religion?

6. What makes a person a hypocrite?

7. Do you think hypocrites are aware of their hypocrisy? Explain.

8. Why do you think that Jesus found self-righteousness the most repugnant of sins?

9. List some warnings to Christians that can be found in this lesson.

10. What additional thoughts or ideas from this chapter would you like to explore?

Prayer

Dear God, thank you for this lesson on self-righteousness and on not being entirely truthful. Keep us from falling short of your expectations. Help us be genuine Christians and faithful to your calling. Amen.

5. DID THE APOSTLES MAKE A MISTAKE?

Summary

This chapter explores the similarities, differences and misunderstandings between groups of believers in the early church. It looks at the death of Stephen and how the apostles handled the tough issues facing them.

Questions

1. Discuss the similarities and differences of the two types of Jews in the Jerusalem church.

2. What was the misunderstanding between these two groups?

3. How did the apostles react to this situation?

4. Describe Stephen. What do you admire about him?

5. Give a summary of Stephen's sermon. Why did it trigger his death?

6. So, did the apostles make a mistake? What issues are involved?

7. Discuss the ministry and achievements of Philip.

8. What did Martin Luther say about the priesthood of all believers?

9. How did early Methodism deal with these issues?

10. What additional thoughts or ideas from this chapter would you like to explore?

Prayer

Dear God, thank you for the faith of the early believers and apostles who shaped our church. Help us learn lessons from the life and death of Stephen. May your church continue to face tough issues and learn from past experiences. Amen.

6. THEN THERE WAS PAUL

Summary

This chapter reflects on the life and ministry of Paul. It includes his conversion, his relationship with the church in Jerusalem, and his many accomplishments.

Questions

1. List what we know and do not know about Paul.

2. What role did Paul play in the death of Stephen?

3. Before his conversion, what were his goals?

4. Describe what happened on the road to Damascus.

5. How did Ananias minister to Paul and why?

6. What difficulties did Paul encounter in his ministry after his conversion?

7. Why was Paul's relationship with the Jerusalem Church an uneasy one?

8. Discuss why Paul was sent to Tarsus and why he needed the Tarsus interlude.

9. List some of Paul's accomplishments after his time in Tarsus.

10. What additional thoughts and ideas from this chapter would you like to explore?

Prayer

Dear God, thank you for providing Paul to lead the early church and to show us how to spread the gospel. May we be fearless in our faith and minister to others as best we can. Please be with us through the difficulties we may face. Amen.

7. THE SLOW PROCESS OF TUMBLING WALLS

Summary

This chapter looks at problems in the early church and the roles of Philip, Peter, Cornelius, and others in putting the church on the right path. It shows how the Holy Spirit helped break down walls of prejudice and empowered believers.

Questions

1. Identify and briefly discuss the problematic issue of the early church.

2. How was Judaism different from other religions?

3. What changed with the arrival of Jesus?

4. How were Philip, Peter, and the Holy Spirit significant in this story?

5. What role did Cornelius play?

6. In your own words, give a summary of what Peter says in 11:4.

7. Explain how the Holy Spirit helps break down walls.

8. Give the reasoning for the letter sent out by the official body in 15:29.

9. What can we learn about prejudices and deep convictions from this lesson?

10. What additional thoughts and ideas from this chapter would you like to explore?

Prayer

Dear God, thank you for your leaders who guide our church and struggle with many issues and challenges. Please continue to provide your Holy Spirit to help us as we minister to others. Remind us that we are never alone. Amen.

8. THE MAN WHO SAVED THE NEW TESTAMENT

Summary

This chapter explores the life of Barnabas and his many contributions to the early church. It illustrates the power of humility and encouragement.

Questions

1. Review what you know about Barnabas.

2. How was Barnabas a key person in God's plan?

3. In what way was Barnabas an encourager and a pearl of great price?

4. Discuss why goodness is a key to humility.

5. What did Barnabas know about Saul that others did not?

6. Discuss the nature and outcome of the disagreement between Paul and Barnabas.

7. What insights do three of Paul's letters give about Barnabas beyond Cyprus?

8. Tell about someone who believed in you when you needed it.

9. Share what impresses you the most about Barnabas.

10. What additional thoughts and ideas from this chapter would you like to explore?

Prayer

Dear God, thank you for servants like Barnabas, who responded to your calling and ministered to others. Thank you for providing help when it is needed and resources to move your church ahead. Help us learn from the life of Barnabas the true meaning of service. Amen.

9. THE ANONYMOUS APOSTLES

Summary

This chapter is a tribute to those individuals—often nameless—who provided leadership and ministry to the early church and beyond. It tells us of the many challenges they faced and of their accomplishments.

Questions

1. How and why does the author use the word *apostle* in a controversial way?

2. Name some of the other nine apostles and their regions of ministry, per tradition.

3. What is known about the "pious soldier" who served Cornelius?

4. Why might you consider people who experienced miracles to be apostles?

5. Discuss why Dr. Kalas says that nothing is so contagious as a thoroughly convinced convert.

6. What role did John Wesley play in using converts?

7. Who or what was responsible for early church growth?

8. What does this lesson tell us about today's anonymous apostles?

9. Share which apostle you admire the most and why.

10. What additional thoughts and ideas from this chapter would you like to explore?

Prayer

Dear God, thank you for those who accepted your call to minister to others, known and unknown. Help us remember their service and sacrifices. Guide us as we carry on their work today. Amen.

10. THE IRREDUCIBLE MESSAGE

Summary

This chapter takes us to Athens when the apostle Paul visited the city. It shows the challenges he faced there in sharing the good news of Jesus. The chapter also includes common sermons and messages during this time period, and what motivated these ministers to press forward.

Questions

1. Discuss what Athens was like when Paul visited.

2. What challenges did Christians face when trying to share their faith?

3. Discuss what the apostle told the citizens of Athens.

4. What impresses you most about the ministry of the apostles?

5. Describe the early focus of sermons.

6. Why was Paul's message difficult for the people of Athens to accept?

7. Name some issues covered in letters by the apostles.

8. Why was their message often not an easy sell?

9. List some differences in the Christian message, then and today.

10. What additional thoughts and ideas from this chapter would you like to explore?

Prayer

Dear God, thank you for the timeless message of your love and forgiveness that continues today. Help us continue your ministry to those who need hope and salvation. Grant us the courage to proclaim your word to others, regardless of the challenges faced.

11. THE SHAPING OF DOCTRINE

Summary

This chapter continues to examine the impact of Paul with a focus on the shaping of doctrine. It shows us issues of the times, what people of the Way believed, and why we are indebted to Paul today for his tireless ministry.

Questions

1. Share some reasons for the appeal of Jesus.

2. Why was the apostle Paul unappealing to many?

3. Discuss the author's statement: "If the twenty-first-century church is to regain the wonder of the first century, it must regain its Old Testament roots."

4. Why can't we be a New Testament church without our Old Testament roots?

5. List some difficulties Paul faced in shaping doctrine.

6. How did early Christians view Christ? Name some issues involved.

7. What did people of the Way believe?

8. How and why was the gospel all one piece to Paul?

9. Why could Paul be called the "Grandson of Encouragement"?

10. What additional thoughts and ideas from this chapter would you like to explore?

Prayer

Dear God, thank you for nourishing your church through doctrine, ministers, faithful believers, and the power of your Holy Spirit. Help us learn from the past to minister in the present. Continue to teach and guide us as we move forward. Amen.

12. THE MAPS OF PAUL AND SEVERAL OTHERS

Summary

This chapter is about how the gospel was spread to new lands by the apostles and others. It tells us the sacrifices made, how and why God's message was proclaimed, and how the church continued to grow then as it continues to grow today.

Questions

1. Why are we indebted to Luke?

2. Discuss the beginning of Paul's ministry to the Gentiles.

3. List some of the dangers Paul faced in his ministry.

4. How was Saul (Paul) an unintentional missionary? Why was this a turning point?

5. Name some reasons the church grew.

6. Why was it often difficult to keep the fires of faith alive in people and in churches?

7. How and why has the story of Acts been repeated?

8. Where and why is Christianity growing today in the world?

9. Share a lesson or insight you learned from reading this book.

10. What additional thoughts and ideas from this chapter would you like to explore?

Prayer

Dear God, thank you for this time together. Thank you for insights shared by group members and for giving us the opportunity to learn more about your ministry and the gospel. Please bless us all. Amen.